The Lessons I've Learned

BETTER GOLF THE SAM SNEAD WAY

Sam Snead with Don Wade

Collier Books/Macmillan Publishing Company * New York

Collier Macmillan Canada * Toronto

Maxwell Macmillan International
New York * Oxford * Singapore * Sydney

Macmillan Publishing Company
866 Third Avenue, New York, NY 10022

Collier Macmillan Canada, Inc.
1200 Eglinton Avenue East, Suite 200
Don Mills, Ontario M3C 3N1

Library of Congress Cataloging-in-Publication Data
Snead, Sam, 1912–
    The lessons I've learned: better golf the Sam Snead way/by Sam
Snead with Don Wade.
       p.   cm.
    Reprint. Originally published: New York: Macmillan, c1989.
    ISBN 0-02-037441-0
    1. Golf. I. Wade, Don. II. Title
GV965.S666   1990
796.352'3—dc20   90-47128   CIP

Macmillan books are available at special discounts for bulk purchases for
sales promotions, premiums, fund-raising, or educational use.
For details, contact:
                    Special Sales Director
                    Macmillan Publishing Company
                    866 Third Avenue
                    New York, NY 10022

First Collier Books Edition 1991

10 9 8 7 6 5 4 3 2 1

The Lessons I've Learned is available in a hardcover edition from Macmillan
Publishing Company, a division of Macmillan, Inc.

Printed in the United States of America

Design by Antler & Baldwin, Inc.

For my grandson, Little Sam

Contents

Foreword

BOB HOPE

Mr. Sam Snead
Hot Springs
Virginia 24445

Dear Sam,

    Congratulations on your new book, "Lessons I
Have Learned." If I didn't know it was written
by you I would have thought it was a handbook
authored by electronic preachers.

    If lessons in golf are going to be taught -
you're the master. You're the only professional
golfer to have won official tournaments in six
different decades...using 24 sets of golf clubs,
50 golf bags and one hat. And it has been
reported that you have been playing the game so
long that your first prize money was in confederate
dollars.

    I'm convinced that if golf had not been played
until Sam Snead...you would have invented it.
Afterall, the world knows you weren't born... your
mother found you in a sand trap in Hot Springs,
Virginia.

    You make the game look so easy, now perhaps
with your "lessons" I can learn how you do it.

    Keep swinging, Sam,

                                Bob Hope

BH/jk

arnold palmer

orlando,
florida
32819

Dear Sam:

We have certainly had our share of memorable moments
in golf over the many years that we have known each
other. The first one for me came in that rather
out-of-the-way tournament -- the Panama Open back in
1956 -- when we went head-to-head for six extra holes.
I felt very strongly that I could become a successful
player on the Tour when I turned pro and, when I won
that playoff in my second season against one of the
greatest players in the game, I felt that I had proved
to myself that I could beat the best.

There have been so many other experiences we have shared
over the last 34 years, perhaps the most unforgettable
when we played twice as the team representing the United
States in the Canada Cup Matches and won the championships
for our country in 1960 in Ireland and 1962 in Argentina.

I have always admired your game and its naturalness
and rhythm. I'm sure we all have learned something
from playing with you and against you in a career that
may well never be matched in terms of victories and
longevity.

Sam, I hope that you will continue to enjoy your golf
for many years to come.

                                Sincerely,

                                Arnold Palmer
                                Arnold Palmer

AP/jf

Mr. Sam Snead
Hot Springs,
Virginia 24445

Jack Nicklaus

Dear Sam:

I heard about your new book and wanted to wish you
well. In fact, I felt a couple of comments that I might
make about you might be appropriate for you to use.

In my opinion, you are probably the most gifted natural
athlete the game of golf has known. You played longer--and
better--than anybody who ever played the game. You also
brought the game color and a lot of great golf shots.

I have always enjoyed watching you, and I've sure
learned from you too. I'll never forget playing in the Ohio
State Open when I was 16. I'd been able to arrange an early
starting time for my Friday round so that I could play an
exhibition with you that afternoon in Urbana. You were in
great form! The next day I went back to Marietta, mimicked
your fantastic swing and rhythm, and shot a 64-72 to win the
tournament.

But you know, Sam, it wasn't as long as two years ago
that we played a practice round together, and I watched your
short iron swing with interest. I found myself mimicking
your swing again, all those many years later! You have a
swing for all ages. Golfers will always be trying to copy
and learn it.

You have been a good friend to me, and a great inspira-
tion to many in the game of golf. I hope you play forever!

Best regards,

Mr. Sam Snead
Hot Springs, Virginia 24445

North Palm Beach, Florida 33408

GERALD R. FORD

February 14, 1989

Dear Sam:

Having played more than a few golf games with you
I've done my best to imitate your magnificent
swing. Your helpful coaching was highly
beneficial, but I'm still a struggling 16
handicapper. I will continue to follow your
suggestions. You are the best.

Your long and successful career on the PGA Tour
has established an enviable record for all that
have followed. Congratulations on your countless
contributions to golf all over the world. Golf is
a better game for more players because of your
skill and dedication.

I'm most grateful for our friendship.

Warmest, best wishes,

Mr. Sam Snead
Hotsprings, Virginia 24445

TOM WATSON

GOLF PROFESSIONAL

KANSAS CITY, MISSOURI 64105

Mr. Sam Snead
Hot Springs
Virginia 24445

Dear Sam:

I recall a great lesson that I learned from you. On my
first trip to The Masters, my father, Ray, told me "sit in the
bleachers behind the practice area and watch Sam Snead swing".
It was great advice.

I hope to see that same swing for many years to come.

Sincerely,

Tom Watson

TW:rm

TOM KITE
Austin, Texas

Mr. Sam Snead
Hot Springs, Virginia   24445

Dear Sam:

CONGRATULATIONS ON YOUR BOOK!   I am glad to see you passing along all you know about this great game.

When I remember back to my first couple of years on tour one of my fondest recollections is playing practice rounds together. They were not cheap, but they were educational. There were always situations on the course where you chose to play an entirely different club or shot than I would have. And the repertoire seemed endless. I asked Harvey Penick, the great teacher, if he thought it was possible for a player today to learn all the shots you had and be able to use them in competition. He disappointed me by saying, "probably not." But he explained about all the various conditions you learned to play golf in and how different and improved the conditions are now. So all I could do is watch and marvel and learn from you.

Needless to say, there will never be another Sam Snead and that is as it should be. So I am glad I had the chance to see you play for a few years.

Thanks for the lessons.

Sincerely,

TOM KITE

Acknowledgments

am nead

HOT SPRINGS, VIRGINIA 24445

Hello!

Thanks for picking up my book. This has really been a team effort and I'd like to take a second and thank the people who worked so hard to make it possible.

First, I can't say enough for Ed Barner, who has been my manager and friend for the past 20 years. This book was his idea and he worked tirelessly to make it a reality. He's the best in the business, and if I had known him earlier, I'd have a lot more of those tomato cans full of cash buried in my backyard.

I imagine that over the years, Jim McQueen has drawn more illustrations of me and other golfers than any man alive. He was our only choice for this book, and he came through in the clutch again. The same is true for photographer Steve Szurlej. Not only does he get the job done right, but he gets it right the first time.

I also want to thank Rick Wolff, who edited this book for Macmillan. Even now, he still thinks baseball is a better game than golf, but he'll get over it.

Finally, I want to thank Don Wade. He is unquestionably one of the most gifted writers around. This book is the result of a true and long lasting friendship. We have worked together on stories now for ten years, and that helped make writing this book a pleasure. Of course, that doesn't mean he is going to get any more strokes any time soon.

Cheers!

SAM SNEAD

Introduction

*I*f there is one thing I've learned about golf after all these years, it's that you never really stop learning.

When I was just a little peckerwood of a kid, my first taste of the game came from watching my older brothers, Lyle, Jess, Pete and Homer—especially Homer because he was the best athlete of the bunch and I idolized him. He'd stand out there and just tear the cover off the ball, and that's what I'd do, too.

Over the years people have made it sound as if I fell out of a tree one day, picked up a branch off the ground and hit the first horse chestnut I could find 300 yards. Nothing could be further from the truth. I've been blessed with an athlete's body and I always have enjoyed beating the other guy, but golf has been as much work for me as for the other guy. I will say, though, that it's been a damn sight more fun for me than most people have had in their walk of life.

I was lucky to have been born in the shadow of The Homestead in Hot Springs, Virginia. I started caddying there when I was seven and it gave me a chance to see a lot of golfers, both good and bad. Hot Springs is tucked up in a valley of the Back Creek Mountains near the West Virginia border. It was the perfect place for a youngster to grow up because I could spend my days hunting, fishing, trapping or just being off in the woods. When you spend as much time in the outdoors as I did, you learn to be very observant. All your senses work overtime. It was just natural, then, that when I started caddying and was bitten by the golf bug, I paid careful attention to what was going on around me.

I turned pro in 1934, and honed my skills by giving as many lessons as I could at The Homestead and by playing in local tournaments. But it didn't take long for me to figure out that if I was really going to make something out of myself, I'd have to test myself against the best players in the game. I won my first tournament, the Virginia Closed Professional, in 1936, and a year later I joined the tour.

I believe you can learn from observing both good and bad players, but to really improve, you've got to test yourself against the best competition possible. When I got out on the tour, I made the most of my chances to play with the better players. Just watching fellows like Byron Nelson, Harry Cooper, Paul Runyan, George Fazio and so many others helped me add some polish to my game.

I don't think there's been a competitive round in which I haven't learned something. Maybe it was a swing key that worked for me that I could recall down the road when my game got a little out of whack. Another time it might be a little shot around the green I'd see one of the fellows play. After the round I'd go off and practice it until I felt comfortable enough to try it under pressure—which is the only time you'll know if something really works.

A lot of times, particularly in those early years, the lessons I learned were about myself. I had to learn how to handle being in contention, or how to handle winning and losing.

In those years I'd concentrate so completely that I could go into the locker room during a tournament and tell you which pair of shoes belonged to which player. That's just how intently I studied the other guys. And, as you'll read in the following pages, that concentration paid off under the gun, when I could tell from a player's mannerisms that he was about to crack just enough for me to come away with a win.

Of course, as I've grown older I've had to learn another lesson, and that's how to adjust my total game to the reality that I'm now seventy-six years old. As I told a reporter not so long ago, "I've always played by feel, but sometimes these days all I feel are aches and pains."

So I've had to make some adjustments. I've experimented with different kinds of clubs and balls, trying to hang onto the distance Father Time and lush fairways keep trying to steal from me. Years ago, after battling another case of the "yips," I went to my sidesaddle-style of putting to try and settle my nerves. This past winter, when I went south, I went to work with a physical therapist to try to force myself back into shape so I can go after some of the younger guys on the Senior Tour. As my wife, Audrey, says, the best way to ensure that I'm serious about getting into shape is to pay for it out of my own pocket. At the rates this guy is charging, I'd better come out of these sessions looking like Mr. America.

Some of my friends ask me, why do I bother? After all, I could play golf with my friends, go fishing and hunting, and just enjoy some time away from airports and hassles.

Well, I enjoy the competition and being out there with the other guys. And I believe I can still give them a run for their money because I'm still learning about this game.

Why, just a few years ago I played one of the best rounds of my career, and the story of how I did it will give you a pretty good example of why golf is the greatest game of them all.

Back in the summer of 1983, I was watching a baseball game on television when one of the players said he had been in a batting slump because he hadn't been extending his arms through the ball. Damned if that wasn't like a light bulb going on in my head. I had been hitting the ball poorly and without much zip, and I realized that had been the problem.

The next day I went out for a match with some friends down at the Lower Cascades course at The Homestead. I went out like a house afire and turned the front side in 30 with just thirteen putts. I had a 30 on the back, and it would have been a 59 if I hadn't gotten a bad bounce on my approach to the last green. I'll tell you this, I wish I could have seen my nephew J.C.'s face when he heard about my round. My 60 tied his for the course record, and every time I see my scorecard next to his it brings a little smile to my face.

That round sums up what I love about this game. You never—ever—stop learning. And you never know when that next good round is going to come along and make a couple bucks for you.

If this book can help you do that—no matter how old or how good a golfer you are—then it will have done what I hoped it would do: give you a taste of the enjoyment golf has given me over all these years.

Author's Note

*T*he conventional wisdom holds that if Arnold Palmer didn't invent golf, he at least rocketed it into the modern era. The American people watched Arnold drive the ball off the world, hitch up his slacks, hit a recovery shot that defied logic, take a drag on his cigarette, then knock in an equally impossible putt to win yet another tournament.

Or come up just short. Either way, people imagined that they played the same way Arnie did, and that was that.

Now all that may be true, but for every person who saw himself as a heroic scrambler, I think there were a hell of a lot more who, in their heart of hearts, believed they swung the club with the grace and power and fluidity of Sam Snead. Of course, none of us does. No one else ever has.

Byron Nelson, who was born in the same year as both Sam and

Ben Hogan, once made this observation about Sam's importance to the game's growth:

> Bob Jones was enormously popular and drew people to golf who really didn't know very much about it. Back in the '20s and '30s it was still considered a rich man's sport. After he retired, it was Sam that really caught the public's eye. He played with such grace and power—and he had such an ability to be dramatic—that he had the same effect on the average sports fan. But more than that, Sam was always willing to go out of his way to do clinics and exhibitions or go to the local Rotary Club luncheons and get publicity for our tournaments. We all had to do these, but I think Sam did many more than his share. He always was good copy, and there's really no way to measure how important Sam was to the game's popularity.

I first met Sam eleven years ago. He and Gardner Dickinson had just won the inaugural Legends of Golf, and the stage was being set for the phenomenal—and totally unexpected—birth of the Senior Tour. I traveled to Pinehurst, North Carolina, to meet Sam and do my first piece for *Golf Digest*.

In the years that followed, Sam and I have collaborated on dozens of pieces. I've long been impressed by his candor, insights and memory for places, players and tournaments. And his sense of humor.

One afternoon a few years ago Sam and I sat outside his house in Florida. Across the way was an older man fishing in one of the many ponds and streams that ran through the course.

"The other day I was out fishing and I was wearing a baseball cap instead of my old straw hat," recalled Sam. "That old-timer over there was looking me up and down, trying to figure out just who I was. Finally, he came over, introduced himself and asked if I were someone famous.

" 'Why yes, I expect you might have heard of me,' I replied.

" 'Do you play golf?' the man asked.

" 'That's right,' I said.

" 'I knew it,' said the old-timer. 'You're Ben Hogan.'

"It ruined my whole damned day," said Sam.

One of the pleasures of working with Sam is that I've had the chance to play more matches with him than I can count. The bet is always the same: two a side for $5, $5 and $10. It's a safe bet for Sam: He knows I'm not going to beat him; I know I'm not going to beat him. And he knows I know I'm not going to beat him. And if by some fluke I do win one nine, I'm certainly not going to nick him for the 18-hole match.

Anyway, it didn't take me long to figure out that I was better off losing and losing early. Sam's not one for giving advice to an opponent while the match is alive, but once it's over he's always been generous with his help.

Sam is the most single-minded competitor I've met. People talk about how he hates to part with a buck, but the truth is more complex than that. For him, performing well is a matter of pride.

By my count, Sam has done a dozen or so books in his career. He's kept more writers off welfare than the New Deal's Writers' Project ever dreamed possible. The late Herb Graffis, one of the truly legendary characters in a field filled with them, wrote Sam's first book.

"I was at the 1938 PGA Championship at Shawnee-on-Delaware," he recalled. "I was at the deadline and, of course, I hadn't come close to getting the book done. It was hot and humid in the hotel, so I did the only reasonable thing: I took off all my clothes, draped myself in a towel, and sat down with a typewriter and a case of beer. When I woke up the next morning, the beer was gone and the book was finished."

Happily, it hasn't come to that with this book. It's been fun, and I'm flattered that I got the nod to help Sam look back on the lessons he's learned over his career.

Finally, just a word on that career. People are fond of debating who was the best golfer of all time. Let me try to answer it this way:

First, Sam was one of a small group who were—or are—"players for history." By that I mean players whom people should go out of their way to see, if only just once in their life. My list would include—in no particular order—Gene Sarazen, Harry Vardon, Bob Jones,

Walter Hagen, Byron Nelson, Ben Hogan, Arnold Palmer, Jack Nicklaus, Lee Trevino, Gary Player, Tom Watson, Seve Ballesteros and Sam.

Second, I've always liked the answer that Sam had when he was asked who the greatest player was.

"The great players had one thing in common," he explained. "They all found a way to win. It's like comparing Joe Louis with Ali. I don't know who was the best. All I know is, I wouldn't want to be in the ring with either one of them."

But perhaps the best assessment of Sam's place in the game came from Dave Marr, the 1965 PGA Champion and long-time ABC Sports golf analyst.

"There have been a lot of so-called natural golfers over the years, but Sam is in a class by himself," he said. "Sam is supernatural."

The Lessons I've Learned
BETTER GOLF THE SAM SNEAD WAY

The Fundamentals

*B*y now, I expect most people have heard the story about my debate with Ted Williams, the Red Sox Hall of Famer who was the last major leaguer to hit over .400 for a season.

Ted and I were both managed by the late Fred Corcoran, and we spent a lot of time fishing together. One day we got talking about whether it was harder to hit a baseball or a golf ball. Ted said that hitting a baseball was the toughest act in sports because you were trying to hit a round ball with a round bat and the ball was traveling around 90 miles an hour.

"That may be true, Ted," I told him. "But in golf we have to play our foul balls."

I doubt that I did much convincing that day, but I do believe that golf is the toughest sport. That's one reason I've always tried to reduce it to its simplest level. I never have seen any reason to make things any more complicated than they already are.

Over the years I've seen a lot of theories come and go, and watched a lot of pretty good players ruin their games by listening to every Tom, Dick and Harry who comes along with a new "secret." The fact of the matter is that there are no secrets. If you are going to succeed, you must learn the right fundamentals and then practice them often enough so that they become second nature to you. You'll know you've done that when you can put what you've learned to work in competition.

It's hard to resist listening to someone who is playing well. In my early days on tour, the older guys would try to give me the needle by offering suggestions.

"Sam, if you'd just get rid of the old hook grip of yours, you'd be a lot better off," one would say.

Or "I think you'd be better off if you'd let your right hand control your swing, Sam," another might say.

Well, maybe they thought they were helping, but all they were doing was getting my head so fogged up with ideas that I wasn't sure if I was coming or going. Finally, it occurred to me that I was beating these guys pretty regularly, so maybe whatever I was doing wasn't so bad anyway.

As I told my nephew, J.C., one time when he came back home all excited about some new theory about the swing that was popular on tour, "J.C., the good Lord gave you two ears. There's a time to let the malarkey go in one and out the other, and there's a time to stick a finger in your ear and learn something. Why don't you just stick with what comes naturally to you?"

I've always told people that if they'd just use their common sense, they'd come out ahead of the game. Look at it this way: It takes less than two seconds to make a golf swing, and yet people try to analyze what they do in that time right down to the slightest twitch of a muscle. It's not possible.

It's like the story of the guy who approached Lawson Little during a tournament he was leading.

"Excuse me, Mr. Little," the man asked. "I was wondering whether you inhale or exhale on your downswing."

Well, old Lawson got to thinking about that and barely made contact with the ball for the rest of the round. It cost him the tournament, and if he could have found the guy later, it might have cost the man a lot more than that, as mad as Lawton was.

What I'd like to do in this section is give you the basics—the fundamentals—that will give you a fighting chance at a good swing. You can have all the talent and desire in the world, but if your fundamentals are wrong, your swing will eventually fall apart under pressure. These aren't the glamorous parts of the game. It's like building a house: You can't worry about the finishing touches until you've made a good foundation and built a good frame or that house will be all over the lot come the first good storm.

The Grip

Learning to grip the club properly is the most important but also the most difficult of all the basics. People can talk all they want about this theory and that, but the fact of the matter is your hands are the only part of your body that come in contact with the club.

I remember playing in a pro-am a few years back where one of my partners was spraying the ball all over the course. He had a good swing and pretty fair tempo. Finally, I asked him what he was thinking about when he set up to hit the ball.

"I've been trying to get my hands out of the swing," he said. "My pro says I'm too handsy."

"Well, what the hell are you going to hold onto that club with if you take your hands out of the swing?"

I'm glad to say that sunk in pretty quick, and he went on to help us out just enough so that we could win, which meant a nice trophy for the team and a nice check for me.

The fact is, even the best players have to be very careful about checking their grip because it's so easy to get out of position. Your grip can get a little too strong or weak, your shots begin to spray, and the next thing you know you've made a lot of other changes to try to compensate. From there, it's a tumble straight downhill.

The best example of this very thing was Ralph Guldahl, who was

When it comes to gripping a club, use your common sense. Find the grip you are most comfortable with.

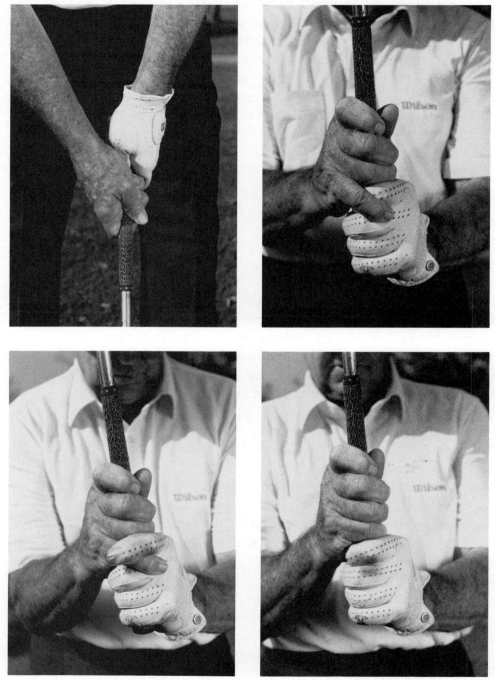

one of the best players in the world when I came on tour. Ralph won the U.S. Open in both 1937 and 1938—in '37 I was sitting on the lead in the clubhouse, sure I had won, when he closed with one of the greatest finishes of all time to beat me. In 1939 he won the Masters, so you can see that we're not talking about any Johnny One-Shot here.

But it seemed as if his game just went away overnight. It's been one of the great mysteries of the sport. It's not that he took to drink or got sick or anything like that. Some people have said that he got a big check to write an instruction book, and for the first time he had to sit down and think about how he played. They figure that got him so screwed up that he could barely lace on his spikes, but I disagree.

Ralph and I played quite a bit together over the years, and his wife finally suggested he ask me for some help. I watched him for a bit, and as soon as I studied his grip, I knew I had found the culprit. He went from having as pretty a grip as you'd ever want to a grip that looked like a damned can full of worms that had gotten loose all over a club.

"Goldie," I said, "where in the world did you get that grip? Why, that's the ugliest thing I've ever seen."

I got him to put his hands back the way they'd been in his glory days, and he did play pretty well for a spell. But sure enough, pretty soon he was back to the poor grip.

"I tried it, Sam, but it just doesn't feel right and I can't stick with it," he said.

And I'm afraid to say, Goldie was never heard from again in terms of winning tournaments. It was a damn shame.

A Few Guidelines

Remember what I said before about common sense? Well, let me ask you this: Where do you think you have the most feel and strength in your hands? I hope your answer was in your fingers.

Look at it this way: If someone handed you a tennis ball and told you to throw it, where would you hold the ball? You wouldn't place it in your palm. If you did, you wouldn't be able to throw it with any power or accuracy. The same is true for gripping the club. You need to grip it in your fingers.

I use the same example when I try to get people to understand how tightly they should grip the club. If you held a ball with a tight, vise-like grip, how well would you be able to throw it? Not very well. Just watch a pitcher in baseball. Those fellows get the ball out on their fingertips—where the feel is—and hold it just tight enough to control it.

I've always said that you should grip a club with the same pressure you'd use to hold a little bird in your hand. You don't want it to fly away, but you don't want the bird's eyes to come popping out of its head, either. Most of the players I see would be hell to pay on a little bird.

As for the type of grips, there are three to choose from, but the most popular is the Vardon, or overlapping, grip, where the little finger of your right hand fits into the slot formed by the first two fingers of your left hand. Notice that I said it fits into the slot between the fingers. Too often I see people putting their little finger right over the left forefinger. The idea is to get your hands working together as a unit, and my way helps you do that a little bit better.

The second grip is the interlocking grip. With this grip, you simply interlock the forefinger of the left hand with the little finger of the right.

This is a pretty good grip for people with smaller or weaker hands, since it does help get the club into the fingers a little easier, and it also helps your hands work together as one.

My feeling, though, is that you have to give up a little bit of feel, since your left forefinger is off the club. Still and all, any grip used by players like Gene Sarazen, Jack Nicklaus and Tom Kite can't be too bad, and if, like them, you have small hands, this grip might be worth a try. Just remember, like any experiment or change in golf, you have to make sure you have it right, and then give yourself plenty of time to give it a fair shake.

The last type of grip is called the ten-finger, or baseball, grip. As the name says, you put all ten fingers on the club, which at first sounds as if it should be a pretty good grip. After all, you'd think that with this grip you'd have more feel, power and control.

But I disagree. The biggest problem I see with this grip is that it makes it tough for your hands to work together as one. Instead, what happens is that your right hand tends to take control, and you end up with a whippy, hinging action at impact. That's awfully hard to keep under control.

Bob Rosburg, who won the 1959 PGA Championship, was one of the few players I know who played with this grip. Rossie had tremendous natural feel and talent, and he just played so much with this grip as a kid that he never could get comfortable with making a change. That was fine for him, but not many people have his talent—or the time it took him to get the most out of this type of grip.

While it is true that making a grip change is hard work, the good news is that it is something you can do at home, in any kind of weather. Instead of just lying back on the couch to watch television, why not sit in an easy chair with a club, gripping and regripping it until you become comfortable with the feel of a correct grip?

The Stance: Building a Solid Base

I've always believed that a good golf swing is built from the bottom up. I still work very hard to make sure that all the parts of my body—my legs, arms, hands and shoulders—work at the same pace, and I control that pace or tempo with my footwork. If one element gets out of whack, I'm in for a long day.

In later sections we'll deal with footwork and how you can learn to use your feet and legs to monitor the pace of your swing. I mention it here because it is one reason learning a proper stance is so important. Without a good stance you can't make a decent weight shift, and that will cost you both power and accuracy.

The correct stance width is one that is wide enough to support your body throughout the swing, yet narrow enough to allow you to make a good pivot and weight shift. For as long as I can remember, people have been taught that the correct width is shoulder width apart, and that's not a bad rule. The problem is that your stance should change from shot to shot.

My rule of thumb is that the longer the club, the wider the

stance. It stands to reason that you need a wider stance to support the speed and motion of a driver swing than you do to support a 5-iron swing. It's also true that the longer the club, the more weight you need behind the ball at impact. For example, a driver is hit with a sweeping, level blow while a short iron is hit with a crisply descending blow. To accomplish this, it stands to reason that your ball position must vary throughout the bag. For a driver, I position the ball off my left heel. As I work my way down through the set, the ball position moves steadily back, so that my short irons are played from the middle of my stance. The only time I play a shot any farther back than the center of my stance is if I have a shot from either a downhill or sidehill lie, which will cause my swing to bottom out sooner than it would from a level lie.

While my ball position varies, the distance I position the ball from my body remains the same for each club. Byron Nelson once said, "Nobody stands too close to the ball," and he was pretty much right on the money. People naturally stand too far from the ball because it gives them a feeling of freedom or power. The truth is, standing too far from the ball causes you to lunge out of position on the downswing, as the motion pulls your weight forward, out over your toes.

I tell people that if, when they address the ball, they can just barely pass their hand between their hips and the butt end of the club, then they have the ball in a pretty good position.

Not only does the ball position vary from club to club, but your stance gradually becomes more open as the clubs become shorter. For example, when I'm hitting a driver, fairway wood or long iron, I play from a square stance. That is, if you drew a line from my left toe to my right toe, it would parallel the target line. As the clubs get shorter and their lies become more upright, my swing naturally becomes more vertical, so my stance becomes more open, with the left foot pulled back away from the target line.

Later, in the shotmaking chapter, I'll discuss how you should vary your stance to either draw or fade the ball, but right here I'd like to give you one last tip on your stance: Too often people are told to play from a square stance, and they think this means that their feet should set up squarely—or at a 90-degree angle—to the target line. In truth, almost all the good players angle their left foot out slightly. In other words, they turn their toes toward the target. This helps them release their body fully at impact, as well as giving them a slightly broader, more secure base to swing from.

I like to suggest that players—especially older people—who have a tough time making a good, full pivot on the backswing, toe out their right foot as well. This little correction will not only help you turn more easily, but it will also help prevent your weight from getting to the outside of your right foot, which can lead to swaying.

Footwork— ## The Forgotten Fundamental

I can't think of a sport in which footwork doesn't play a big role. A boxer who has lead feet is destined to spend a lot of time looking at the ceiling. A pitcher or quarterback won't have much zip on the ball if he throws flat-footed, and if you show me a batter who swings from his hips, without a good stride, I'll show you a boy who is headed for the bush leagues.

And yet footwork is largely overlooked by golfers, who are consumed by all sorts of theories and gimmicks. As I said earlier, I think you swing from the ground up, and let your legs and feet control the pace of your swing.

Gene Sarazen once credited me with starting something called "The One-Piece Swing." Well, I don't know that I started it, but I'm a big believer in all the parts of the swing moving in unison, back and forth, to and fro.

If you remember from earlier in this book, I said that I believe in keeping this complicated game as simple as possible, and that's especially true when it comes to the swing. There may be some people who have enough coordination to move their legs at one speed, their arms at another, their hips and shoulders at a third and the club at a fourth, but I've never run across the guy.

I want everything moving together, and it stands to reason that my legs have to control the pace because they are the big muscles. I just can't move my legs as fast as I can move my arms, so everything has to follow the pace my legs set.

Years ago I was giving a lesson to a fellow who struck me as the most uncoordinated person I'd ever seen. Every part of his body moved at a different speed. Finally, I asked him if he knew what waltz time was.

"I certainly should," he said. "After all, I'm a dance instructor."

"Well hell," I told him. "Why don't you just hum your favorite waltz and swing to the beat of the tune?"

The difference was like night and day. He swung in the sweetest, most coordinated and controlled way you could imagine.

In fact, swinging the club to a waltz tune is one of my secrets under pressure, and it might just be a good way for you to practice and find a rhythm that works for you.

I have a couple other thoughts that might help you develop or improve your footwork.

A big problem that I see among many amateurs is that they have a tendency to overdo instruction. It's like the old saying, "A couple aspirin might cure what ails you, but the whole bottle will probably kill you."

You need to guard against swaying during your swing, since that allows your weight to get to the outside of your feet. This is especially true on the backswing.

To prevent this, I urge people to swing on the "insides" of their feet. In other words, try to roll off the inside of your left foot on your backswing, and then roll off the inside of your right foot on the downswing. In the beginning it's a good idea to practice this without a club or ball. Just make a swing with your arms, swinging back and forth, back and forth, to a 1-2, 1-2 count.

Here's a second tip that may help you swing from the insides of your feet and keep your weight centered more throughout your swing: Try to play knock-kneed. Let me explain.

A few years back Ben Hogan wrote an instruction book in which he talked about his feeling that when he swung the club he tried to imagine that his arms were held together by a belt. That made sense to me, and the more I thought about it, the more I realized that I did something similar with my legs.

When I address the ball, I pinch my knees in just a little. Doing this helps get my weight centered over the inside of my feet, and it also keeps my legs working together. Remember, the key to this is that my knees are *slightly* together. Don't overdo it, but do give it a try.

The Secret to Aiming

There's not many things more frustrating in golf than making a good swing, only to have the ball land in jail because you didn't aim properly.

The truth is, most people miss shots to the right most of the time—and not because they slice the ball, either. It's just human nature that when you set up to the ball and look down at the target, you tend to aim where your *eyes* are looking instead of where the club is aimed. As a result, shot after shot is missed to the right or pulled back to the left as players try to compensate for a problem that can be fixed if you learn—and follow—what is called a pre-shot routine.

Everyone has a slightly different routine, but all good players have one they follow on every shot. And while the routines vary, we all do pretty much the same things.

After studying my lie and the shot I'm facing, I pull the club from the bag and stand directly behind the ball, facing the target.

I visualize the shot—and I'll get into this in more detail in the shotmaking chapter—then I select an intermediate target. This target can be a divot, a piece of grass, anything that is a foot or so in front of the ball on a line between the ball and the target. *This* is the target I align the clubface with. It stands to reason that it's easier to aim at a target a foot from the ball than it is a target that is hundreds of yards away.

A word of warning here: You can pick anything you like as an intermediate target, but you can't place anything down to do the job. That's against the rules.

Once I've picked the target, I walk into my address position from the side, placing the clubhead down behind the ball on a line with my intermediate target. Now I can build my stance around the club, confident that my club and my body are aimed properly. I place my left foot in position first, then the right. I build my stance off my left foot.

The difference between my routine and the way I see many weekend players set up to a shot, is that I pick an intermediate target to help me aim and then I build my stance around the clubface. Too often amateurs will take their stance and then try to aim the clubface—and when they do, they almost always aim out to the right.

One last piece of advice on aiming: Once you're in position, it's a good idea to look back to your target, but when you do, rotate your head back and forth. The most common mistake I see is people lifting their head to look at the target, then lowering it again to look at the ball. This causes your body to raise and lower, and can cause you to work your way out of position.

Starting the Swing

Until this point, I've dealt with what I'll call the pre-swing fundamentals. In a later section we'll cover the different swing keys I've used throughout my career to keep my swing in the groove. But right here, I'd like to touch on actually getting the swing started.

In one respect, golf is almost unique because it is one of the few sports where you *act* instead of *react*. Tennis players or batters or basketball players don't really have time to think how they are going to begin their pitch or shot or whatever. Their instincts take over and they perform.

But in golf, you have to pull the trigger, which is one reason you see so many so-called dubs freeze over the ball. They are running a long list of dos and don'ts through their mind, then, once they figure they can't put it off any longer, they get started—usually one way one time and another way the next.

This puts them behind the eight ball before they have a fighting chance. Why? Because the first two feet of the swing are the most crucial. They determine the pace of the swing; the swing arc and path; the width of the swing arc, which, in turn, goes a long way toward determining how much clubhead speed your swing will produce.

My first piece of advice is to keep moving. All good athletes in any sport follow the same rule. Watch a tennis player about to receive serve. He's watching the ball, but he's constantly moving. Same with a batter in baseball.

In golf, the answer is to waggle the club, moving it away and back to the ball for a few feet. This helps you get the feel for taking the club away from the ball, and also keeps your muscles loose and relaxed.

Once you're ready to go, I always teach a person to use what I call a forward press. It's just a little movement that tells your body that the swing is under way. In my case, I kick my right knee slightly to the left, and at the same time I slide my hands ever so slightly to the left. Then, without pausing, I push the clubhead away from the ball. I like to feel that I'm pushing away with my left hand in control. My right hand is just along for the ride. My only effort is to keep the club moving straight away from the ball, low and slow, for the first two crucial feet.

I want to again stress that it is important for every part of my body to work in unison, especially at the start of the swing.

As the club moves back, my weight begins to shift to my right foot, so that by the time the clubhead has passed my right foot, most of my weight has already shifted.

Since my left arm is moving the club straight back from the ball, both my hips and my shoulders are turning very naturally. I don't have to try to turn them. Everything is moving in unison.

People often talk about a quick wrist cock, but I don't like to see it, since it usually leads a person to jerk the club back inside the target line too quickly, and the rhythm of the swing is destroyed before you even give it a chance.

I'll tell you who had to guard against this all the time: President Eisenhower. He'd snatch that club back inside and then get to swinging so quickly that he didn't have a chance of making a decent turn.

One day when I was playing with him, he complained that he had lost a lot of distance.

"Well, Mr. President," I said, summoning my courage. "You've got to get a little bit more of your behind into the shot. You've got to turn, turn and turn some more."

Well, the Secret Service men might have been a bit shocked by my message, but it didn't bother Ike at all.

"Sam, that's just what my pro at Augusta, Ed Dudley, tells me all the time."

Once Ike got to turning instead of snapping that old driver around his body, he picked up a lot of that distance he'd lost over the years.

If this sounds as if it might be your problem, or if you've been spraying the ball all over the lot, here's a drill you can try: Address a ball with your 5-iron and put a second ball down behind your clubhead. Now concentrate on rolling the second ball straight away on the backswing, then hitting the first ball down the practice range. Keep this up until you can do it with a driver. I think you'll find that you hit the ball a lot straighter, and with a lot more distance, than you ever thought possible. Just remember: Low, slow and straight back from the ball—and keep all the parts moving together.

My 85 Percent Solution

Since we've just spent a fair amount of time talking about how the first two feet do so much to determine the pace of your swing, I'd like to take just a little more space and explain what I call My 85 Percent Solution.

When I was a kid, I tried to knock the cover off every ball I hit. But it didn't take me long to figure out that distance was good only if the ball was in play. So from that point on, I promised that I'd never swing so hard that I'd lose my feel for the club.

I figure that if I swing at about 85 percent of my full speed, it still gives me enough power, but more importantly, it gives me enough control so that I make solid contact most of the time—and solid contact is more important to distance and accuracy than pure power.

Not only that, but by swinging within myself, I have a chance to correct a swing that feels funny to me. Occasionally, for example, my

Try my 85 percent solution. It gives you enough power, but also allows you to make solid contact. That's the key.

2

3

4

5

6

7

8

9

10

11

12

13

14

15

16

17

timing gets a little off and I can feel myself out of position, usually by coming over the top on my downswing. Since I'm not going at the ball full bore, I still have a split second to try to recover. I still might not hit a perfect shot, but at least I'll be able to salvage enough so that the ball is still in play.

That may not sound like much to you, but it's saving a little bit here and a little bit there that helps win tournaments. As the fellow says, golf's a game of minimizing your mistakes.

The Players I've Known
The 1930s and 1940s

I've been very lucky throughout my career. I've known and played with most of the game's greatest and most interesting players. I've divided these players into different generations, and this section will deal with the players I met when I first left Virginia and went out on tour.

I don't have any intention of ranking these players. As I've said so often, you can't honestly compare players unless they competed against one another in their primes, and that's not the case very often.

I think these three sections will have value because I will try to describe each player's strengths and weaknesses. As Lee Trevino once said, the good Lord didn't give anyone every shot with every club. The most successful players have been those who did the most with what they had. To the extent that these sections help you do the same, they will be successful.

Jimmy Demaret   Jimmy was one of the most beloved and, at the same time, most underrated players of all time. I think he had a lot to do with the game's growth among the so-called average Joes through the force of his personality and his sense of humor.

I remember the time when he appeared on the television game show *What's My Line?* The idea of the show was that the guest would come in and the audience, both in the studio and at home, would be told the person's occupation or claim to fame. A panel of blindfolded celebrities would try to guess what the guest did by asking a series of questions.

In Jimmy's case, it took the panel only about a minute. It seems that when he arrived at the studio he walked around introducing himself to everyone he met, saying "Hi, I'm Jimmy Demaret, a professional golfer." Of course, he wound up introducing himself to everyone on the panel, but what the hell, that was just Jimmy's way, whether a guy was a prince or a pauper.

If Jimmy were alive today, his theme song would have been "Don't Worry, Be Happy" because that's just the way he lived. Years ago all the players in the Masters used to stay at the old Bon-Air Hotel. One year I was awakened at two-thirty in the morning by Jimmy wandering down the hall, singing at the top of his lungs. And he had a pretty good voice, too. He used to sing in nightclubs to make a little walking-around money.

Jimmy won three Masters, and people always thought that was pretty amazing, since he did it without practicing. I thought it was even more amazing because he did it without sleeping.

Ben Hogan greatly admired Jimmy and always said he was one of the best players he ever saw. Jimmy was very much a hands player, and he was quick. He'd set up to the ball with that narrow stance of his, take a look at the target and "bang," the ball was gone. I think Ben liked him because he never took Ben too seriously, and Ben appreciated that. It helped Ben relax.

Of course, Jimmy was the guy who really added color to golf clothes. His dad had been a house painter, and Jimmy always said that was where he got his feel for colors. When I first came out on tour, everyone wore a lot of grays and browns, but Jimmy changed all that. There wasn't a color he wouldn't wear, sometimes all at once.

One time we did an exhibition tour through South America, and I'll never forget our arrival as long as I live. The people there were very conservative dressers. If you wore a pin-striped suit, you were considered a pretty flashy bird. Jimmy showed up wearing a yellow and white cap with a little brush stuck on the side, cream-colored pants with a bright red stripe running down the side, a maroon knit shirt, and a pair of white and pink shoes.

Well, I'll tell you, those macho Latins took one look at Jimmy and their eyes bulged clear out of their heads. They didn't know whether to shake his hand or head for the hills. They had never seen anything quite like him. Neither had I. Jimmy never let too much bother him, but he had a run-in with Bob Jones and Clifford Roberts, who ran the Masters, and I don't think he ever quite got over it.

Ben Hogan came up with the idea for the annual champion's dinner, where the defending champion hosts a quiet little get-together for all the past champions. In the course of the dinner, we all exchange stories and jokes and do a lot of catching up, but we also discuss suggestions for how the Masters, or Augusta National, could be improved.

As a general rule, the folks who run the show at Augusta are pretty good about taking advice, which is one reason the Masters is the best tournament in the world. But one year Jimmy suggested that we open the dinner up to the public. That was just his way—the more the merrier.

Neither Bob nor Cliff thought much of the idea, so it was pretty much dismissed. But somehow the newspapers got wind of it, and that set Bob and Cliff right off the world. Bob sent Jimmy a very stern letter, in effect reminding him of how important the Masters had been to his career.

Jimmy was crushed, and he never came back to Augusta until after Bob Jones died. It was one of the rare times when I think Bob Jones acted out of character, and it was a damn shame.

When Jimmy died, it stunned a lot of people. He was one of those guys you just assumed would be around forever. His wife was worried that she'd have to find a job to make ends meet, and she mentioned that to Jackie Burke, who was Jimmy's closest friend.

"Work?" Jackie said to her. "Why, Jimmy has money in every bank in Houston."

That's just the way he was. Money could come and money could go, but Jimmy never changed, and people loved him for that.

Walter Hagen   Walter was a lot like Jimmy Demaret. He genuinely liked people and enjoyed being around them. Also, like Jimmy, he had a reputation as a big party guy, but they both could nurse one drink all night.

Walter had a lot of talent, but his greatest strength was that he was unflappable. He never once panicked on the course, and he was at his best in match play, when he could really go to work on his opponent.

One time he was playing this fellow who had tremendous arms. His arms were so big that he had to roll his sleeves up around his shoulders so he could swing. Walter took one look at him and said, "My God, Mike, those muscles are really something. I'm going to be away all day." And just to make sure that he was, he hit a ton of 3-woods off the tees, while Mike tried to knock the cover off the ball. The trick was that he'd always hit his approach shots first, and generally hit them pretty close. The match didn't last long.

He faced Leo Diegel in the finals of the 1926 PGA Championship, which was a match play championship until 1958. Late the night before, he ran into a friend of his. "Walter, what are you doing up?" his friend asked. "Leo has been in bed since nine o'clock."

"Yes," said Walter, "but he hasn't been sleeping."

The next day Walter began the match by giving Leo a 3-footer on the first hole. Now Leo was one of the worst short putters in history, and worse than that, he knew it. As Walter kept on giving him short putts, he kept wondering what the hell was going on. He found out on the 13th hole, when Walter made him putt a 2-footer. The ball never got near the hole, and that was all she wrote. Walter beat him, 5&3.

Walter was a master at gamesmanship because he understood human nature. Everything he did was aboveboard. And it was effective.

Ben Hogan   I suppose that Ben and I have been more or less thrown together in history because of our so-called rivalry.

The truth is, I always liked Ben and I always liked to win when we played against each other. That meant we never were going to be real close, but on the other hand, we always got along off the course, and I always liked playing with him.

First of all, Ben was easy to play with. He'd wish you luck on the first tee and then he'd go about his business and let you go about yours. The most he might say is, "I believe you're away."

I'd never watch Ben swing because his tempo was so much faster than mine that I was afraid it might throw me off. People have tried to say I didn't watch Ben because I didn't like his swing. That's not true. He had a good swing and it worked just fine for him. It was just a question of tempo.

Ben always was pretty much of a loner, and to some degree that's how you have to be if you're going to be a champion. Golf's a pretty jealous game. She doesn't like you sharing your attentions. I do know Ben had a pretty tough childhood, and I think that may have made him a little more withdrawn than most. Maybe that's one reason he liked Jimmy Demaret as much as he did. Jimmy made him laugh and never really wanted anything from Ben.

Ben was very intense. I roomed with him one time, and he woke me in the middle of the night by grinding his teeth. Grind, grind, grind. I'd never heard anything quite like it.

The next day I mentioned it to Jimmy Demaret, but he said not to worry about it. "That's just Ben sharpening his blades for today's round."

When Ben first came out on tour, he had a very long swing, and he was prone to hitting the occasional hard running hook. He'd have good rounds, but it seemed that at least once every tournament he'd post a "Red Grange"—a 77 or so—that would knock him out of the box.

I give him a lot of credit, though. He stuck with it and taught himself a swing he could trust under pressure. And I give his wife, Valerie, a lot of credit, too. She stood by him in the tough times.

Ben won two PGA Championships—1946 and 1948—at match play, but I don't think he really enjoyed it. He preferred medal play, where he could pick the score he needed to shoot and plan his round accordingly. Ben could really think his way around a course, maybe as well as anyone in history. And he could control his emotions better than anyone, with the possible exception of Jack Nicklaus.

Because Ben is somewhat reclusive, a lot of myths have grown up around him. I don't think he's done much to discourage them, which is fine. More power to him.

I remember one year at the Masters when some of the writers came in all excited about watching Ben play.

"He's like a machine," one of them said. "He's playing his second shots from the same divot marks he made yesterday."

"Well, Ben's smarter than that," I said, getting up to leave. "Why doesn't he just aim a little to the left or the right and get a decent lie?"

Ben could also be one of the most contrary people you'd ever meet. Once he made up his mind there was no point in arguing with him. I'll give you a perfect example:

Ben, Byron Nelson and I were all born in 1912, which is pretty amazing if you consider the odds on one year producing three top players. Anyway, when we turned seventy-five, a fellow came to us with a proposition. He'd pay us $50,000 each to sit down and be interviewed for a videotape. Byron and I both agreed, but Ben balked, so I agreed to give him a call.

"Ben," I said, "you must not have read the fine print. They're offering us $50,000 for a day's talking. We'll come to Fort Worth. We'll come to your office. We'll come to your house. We'll go wherever you want. I don't know about you, but I'm pretty sure Byron could use the money, and I'm not one to let 50 fly out the window."

Well, true to form, Ben had made up his mind and there was no changing it. He just didn't want to be bothered. All I know is, $50,000 can help most folks put up with a lot of bother, but not Ben.

As I say, I like Ben and I'm glad that if I had to have a rival, it was him. You always want to test yourself against the best, and I was fortunate that I got to go up against Ben in our primes.

Bobby Jones Bob was in a class by himself. He was a true gentleman in every part of his life. I suppose the highest compliment you can pay a man is to say that you'd like your son to grow up and be just like him, and that's certainly how I feel about Bob Jones.

There are a lot of misconceptions about Bob. Like anyone else, he had a fair amount of growing up to do. He just didn't hit the world as "Bobby Jones, Hero." In fact, he was the first to admit that he was a snotty little thing as a kid, with one hell of a temper to go along with a wonderful talent. But if you give me the choice between a a kid with a little fire and a placid, well-behaved one, I'll take the one with some spark. I've always said, show me a good loser and I'll show you a seldom winner.

Bob was very well educated, and people just naturally assumed he came from a lot of money, which wasn't the case. His family was comfortable, but he never really made any money until he quit his competitive career in 1930, at age twenty-eight. In fact, I always thought that was one reason he hung up his spikes, so to speak. He had proven everything he wanted to prove, and had to get on with making a living.

It's difficult for people to appreciate just how totally draining golf is at the level Bob Jones played. People know how Byron Nelson used to suffer from a bad stomach in competition, but they don't realize that Bob suffered much the same way. He'd lose ten pounds over the course of a championship, and he wasn't all that big to begin with. That kind of pressure will take its toll on anyone, and it finally took its toll on Bob. Toward the end of his career, even he got a taste of the yips, or the twitchies as the British call them. It happens to everyone who puts his nerves under the gun often enough.

Bob and I played three times after his retirement from competition, but before he was afflicted with a spinal disease that finally took his life. He was a beautiful driver and played fairway woods about as well as anyone ever did. It goes without saying that he was a brilliant

The Players I've Known (1930s–1940s)

Top: Walter Hagen, Paul Runyan, Ben Hogan
Bottom: Bobby Jones, Jimmy Demaret, Bobby Locke, Byron Nelson

Players I've Known (1950s–1960s)

Top: Ray Floyd, Gary Player, Arnold Palmer
Bottom: Jack Nicklaus, Doc Middlecoff, Peter Thomson, Lee Trevino

putter and had an outstanding touch around the greens, but because he drew everything, he wasn't a particularly good long iron player. In fact, if you go back over the record, you'll see that his scores were much worse on the par 3s than on the par 5s. He had a tough time getting to pins that were tucked to the right.

If you think about it, Augusta National is set up for a player like Bob Jones. The par 3s are where you can lose the tournament, but the par 5s are where you can win it because three of the four are reachable for longer hitters, which gives them a potential twelve-shot edge over the field over four rounds.

People always say that golf is different from other big-time sports because it is a "gentleman's game." I think that's because young golfers coming along still look up to players like Bobby Jones as examples of how they should act, both on and off the course—and he was a true gentleman.

Bobby Locke   I guess Bobby Locke was the best putter I ever saw, and maybe the most unorthodox. He hooked everything he hit, from his driver to his putter. I played a series of exhibitions with him in South Africa, his home, on some of the toughest greens you'd ever want to see, and he never three-putted once.

When we finished the exhibitions, Bobby asked me if I thought he should try his luck in the States. I told him the same thing I'd tell any foreigner—you've got to test yourself against the best players in the game, and that's on our tour. That was true then and it's still true today, despite what some writers and promoters would have you believe.

Well, Bobby came over and did pretty well for himself. Clayton Heafner took one look at him and told Jimmy Demaret that Bobby could beat their best ball. I'm not sure he was that good, but if he'd been more comfortable over here, he could have done very well for himself.

Bobby had a puffy little body, a bad grip, a swing that only let him hit the ball with a big hook, and yet he won. If he came along today, some teacher would try to get him to become more "normal," so to speak. If the teacher had succeeded, Bobby would have been ruined.

You've got to let a person live with his or her own little quirks as much as possible.

Byron Nelson   Like Bob Jones, Byron had an outstanding career but retired at a young age. I think that was due partially to nervous exhaustion and partially to the fact that he had won about everything he wanted to win. But more than that, he was totally devoted to his late wife, Louise, and I think she longed to be back home in Texas and get going on the ranch they had been saving to buy.

Byron was a hell of a player, much better than people recognize today. I think he was a better long iron player and driver than Ben, with whom he is often compared because they started out together as caddies. I do think Ben was better around the greens.

Byron is a very gentle man, but he has a streak of steel. He was a very tough competitor but very fair. When he was playing well, he kept pretty much to himself, but when he got off his game, he became more talkative.

One thing that Byron is noted for is his willingness to take young players under his wing. The two who come quickest to my mind are Ken Venturi and Tom Watson. He helped make both of them first-class golfers, and I always thought it made more sense for a kid to seek out someone who had tested his theories under pressure. How in the world can someone tell you what will work under the gun if he's never been there? Byron has been there, and he did as well as any man ever did.

Paul Runyan   I don't suppose anyone ever got more out of his golf game than Paul Runyan. He is a small person, but he managed to develop a swing that let him get every inch out of a shot. But where he excelled was around the greens. He could get the ball up and down from a manhole.

Paul whipped me, 8&7, in the finals of the 1938 PGA Championship at Shawnee-on-Delaware. I'd outdrive him by 30 yards, but I was a basket case on the greens. "Little Poison," on the other hand, made everything he looked at.

That someone of Paul's size could do as well as he did, shows what a great game this is. A good short game is the great equalizer, if you are willing to work at it. It not only saves you strokes, but it can also demoralize your opponent in a hurry—as I found out in 1938.

My Swing Keys
... and Yours

Like most successful golfers, I've developed a number of swing keys over the years. These are reminders—some physical, some mental—to help me keep my swing in the groove from one round to the next.

Your body changes from day to day. Maybe you're just a touch lighter or heavier than the last time you played. Or maybe it's just a question of feel, which comes and goes with all of us.

Whatever the reason, it helps to have a set of keys that you can fall back on to keep your swing in shape, or to help you keep the wheels on when your game begins to fall apart in the middle of a round.

Someone once asked Bobby Jones what his favorite swing key was, and after thinking about it for a second, Jones said, "Whatever worked best, last."

As usual, he was right on the money. The truth of the matter is that nothing ever stays the same in golf. Just when you think you've got it all figured out, the game jumps up and reminds you that you haven't begun to figure it out at all. And that's when your swing keys can help.

Before I begin a round, I always go to the practice tee and warm up. I want to stretch and loosen my muscles, but it's even more important that I find out what key or two is going to work for me that day. Notice that I said "key or two." Your brain just can't handle more than that without becoming confused, defeating the purpose of the keys in the first place.

I've divided my keys into three categories: hand keys, body keys and timing keys. Some of the specific keys will sound familiar because I've touched on them in some of the earlier sections of this book. They are worth repeating, though.

My Hand Keys

Keep a Light Grip Pressure   Tension is a killer in the golf swing, and nine times out of ten tension starts when you grip the club too tightly. I said earlier that you want to grip the club about as tightly as you'd hold onto a little bird. There are several reasons for this. First, if you start squeezing the rubber out of the grip, what chance do you have for finding any feel? Not much. Second, when you grip the club too tightly, you can feel the muscles tighten right up through your arms and even into your shoulders. It's tough to make a nice, flowing swing when your arms are as hard as boards. Finally, it's only natural that your hands are going to tighten up automatically during the swing because the force of gravity will increase the weight of the club as it picks up speed on the downswing.

Put Your Hands in a "Holster"   One thing that all good golfers work very hard on is their consistency. They want to try to make the same swing each time. But like anything else, it's tough to make a repeating swing if you vary your position at address from swing to swing. One fault I see in a lot of amateurs is in the position of their hands at address. One time they'll have their hands way out in front of the ball and the next time they'll try something different and set their hands back.

Sure, there are rare times when you will want to slightly alter your hand or ball position at address in order to hit a specific shot, and we'll get into that a little later. But for right now I want to concentrate on my keys for most shots.

When I set up to the ball, I like to imagine that I'm sliding my hands into a holster positioned just over my left instep. From this position you could draw a straight line down from my left shoulder, through my left arm and right down the club to the ball. That's the position I want to be in at impact, so it just makes sense that it's where I should be at address.

The other advantage that this key gives me is that it helps me feel that my hands are working together as a team. People talk about golf being a left- or right-handed game, but I think it's a whole lot simpler game if you just think about your two hands working together.

Push—Don't Pull—the Club Away from the Ball   At impact, you want to have the club moving squarely into the ball, so it just makes sense to me that when you take the club back away from the ball to begin the swing, you want to take it back straight away from the ball for the first foot or so. The best way I know to ensure this is to push the clubhead away from the ball with both hands working together. While you want both hands working together, it helps to feel that you are pushing the club away with your left hand. If the right hand takes over, there's a tendency to pull the club back to the inside of your target line. In order to get your swing back on track, you must make adjustments later on in your swing if you hope to make solid contact.

By pushing the clubhead back straight away from the ball, you are also setting the pace of your swing at a nice smooth speed. You want to constantly remember, "low and slow" for the first foot or two of the swing. If you jerk the club back away from the ball, you've established a quick rhythm that is hard to overcome.

The other advantage to pushing the clubhead away from the ball is that it naturally turns your shoulders and hips to the right, and helps shift your weight to the right side. People often ask which part of the body begins the backswing, and my answer is always that you turn all the parts together. If one part of your body gets out of whack, then your swing is bound to be uncoordinated, and while you may hit the occasional good shot, the law of averages is working against you.

Finally, your left arm determines the width of your swing arc, and swing arc as much as anything else determines how much clubhead speed you can generate. Think of the clubhead as a rock that is tied to the end of a string. Which will give that rock more hitting power, a one-foot piece of string or a two-foot piece? I hope your answer was the two-foot length.

Let Your Wrists Cock Naturally   For some reason that I've never really understood, the wrist cock is one of those things that some golfers seem to spend a lot of time analyzing, when the truth is it's a natural reaction to the weight of the swinging golf club. Now it's true that some players cock their wrists earlier on the backswing than others. Seve Ballesteros is an example of a player who has an early wrist cock, but in his case I think it's because he learned to play when he was very small, and he needed to cock his wrists early to support the club. Since he was pretty much self-taught, and was successful early on, he just ingrained that into his swing and there's no point in trying to fix something that works as well as his swing does.

My wrists don't really begin to cock until my hands have reached about waist high, which is about the point where I'm no longer pushing the club away from the ball but have begun to lift it into position at the top of my backswing. If you were standing directly behind me, it might even look as if I was pulling my cocked wrists out of my right pants leg pocket.

Set the Club in the Slot   The payoff for a good backswing is the position the club is in at the top of the swing. All good ball strikers, no matter what odd little idiosyncrasies they may have in their swing, get into a good position at the top. I call it the slot.

Take Miller Barber, for example. If you watched his backswing, you wouldn't think he could hit the broad side of a barn, and yet there are damn few players who look better at the top of their swing or who make solid contact more consistently.

When Miller first came out on the regular tour, I asked him why he didn't work on his backswing and eliminate all the loops and hitches.

"I tried to, Sam," he said. "But the more normal I got it, the worse I hit the ball, so I figured I'd better stick with what got me this far."

As far as I'm concerned, the ideal position—the slot—is about halfway between your head and right shoulder. A player with a flatter swing, like Ben Hogan, might set the club a little lower than middle, while a player with a more upright swing, like Jack Nicklaus, sets the club a little closer to his head.

At the top of your swing, you want your hands under the club, and you need to guard against what I call "playing the flute," which occurs when you overswing and lose control of the club with the last two fingers of your left hand.

At the top of the backswing, your club should point at your target. If it is aimed to the left of your target, it is what we call "laid off." If it points to the right of the target, you've "crossed the line."

Here's a simple test to see if you have the club set properly at the top. Swing the club back into the slot, then, without changing the position of the club in your hands, simply bring the club back in front of you. If the shaft points straight up and down, you were in the slot. If it points to the right, you were laid off, and if it points to the left, you crossed the line.

On the other hand, if you do that drill in reverse, you'll be able to find the slot and get the feel for where you should be at the top of your swing.

Hold the club directly in front of you, with your wrists cocked and the club pointing straight up and down. From this position, simply turn your hips and upper body as you would on the backswing, so that your back has turned toward the target. At the same time, set the club in the slot without changing your wrist cock. If you do this correctly, you'll get the feel you've been looking for, without worrying about a lot of cosmic theories.

Once you get the feel for placing the club in the slot, I'd suggest going to the practice tee and trying to hit some shots while concentrating solely on setting the club in the slot. I think you'll like the results.

Start Down with a Pull There's always been a lot of discussion concerning how the downswing is started. Some people argue that it is started by a lateral slide of the hips to the left. Still others believe that it is a turning of the hips, or a planting of the left heel, which often rises off the turf at the completion of the backswing.

All these theories are fine to a degree, but the key that has always worked best for me is beginning the downswing by pulling the club down with the last two fingers of my left hand. This key helps me get the club started down along the proper swing plane, so I can deliver the clubhead to the ball from inside the target line, rather than making the mistake I see so often, which we call "coming over the top."

There's a natural tendency to be in a hurry to hit the ball and control that hitting action with your strongest hand—the right for most people. The problem with this is that it leads to casting the club from the top, much the same way that you would cast a line out with a fishing pole. By doing this, the clubhead is sent outside the swing plane, and unless a correction is made, the club strikes the ball from and outside-to-inside the target line swing path. The results are either a slice or a pulled shot. Coming over the top also leads to a loss of distance, since it causes your wrists, where so much power is stored, to uncock too soon—giving away much of the power you stored on the backswing. By keying on the last two fingers of your left hand, you go a long way toward eliminating the threat of coming over the top, since you've consciously worked on keeping the right hand out of the act until it's needed—at impact, when it can pour on the juice.

The Moment of Truth   Earlier I said that I pay a lot of attention to my address position because that's the same position I want to be in at impact—the clubhead square to the ball and my left arm and the shaft in a straight line.

The truth is, there's just not enough time to think of much of anything at this stage of the game. The clubhead is moving at around 100 miles an hour, so my only thought is to pour on the power with my right hand. But—and this is a big but—you must not let your left wrist break down or collapse at impact. Too often I see players get to this stage of the swing in decent enough shape, only to hit the ball with a flippy, wristy, little flicking action because their left wrist has collapsed at impact.

One key thought that often works for me when I'm trying to get a little extra distance is that the clubhead is chasing the ball right through impact. Of course, it never can catch that little dude, but it's a good thought to have.

Roll Your Hands at Impact   In the previous section I stressed the importance of not letting your left wrist collapse at impact, and that may have caused some of you to wonder what you should do. The answer is to let your wrists roll over.

A good way to get a feel for this sensation is to slide a wooden tongue depressor or a pencil under a watchband on your left wrist so it is resting along the top of your forearm. With this in place, it's not possible for your wrist to bend to the left.

Now grip a club and hold it in front of you, with the shaft pointing up and down. Rotate your wrists so the club points first to the right and then to the left. As you get a feel for this, slowly lower the club so that eventually you are making what amounts to a practice swing or a chipping motion. You can gradually lengthen your swing until it becomes a full swing, but don't try to hit any balls with the tongue depressor or pencil in place.

My Body Keys

Just as I have a set of certain keys that I use for my hands, I also have a set of keys for my body to help remind me of the positions I want my body in both at address and throughout the swing.

Years ago, when I was first learning this game, it was popular to teach people to swing as though they were "swinging in a barrel." I've always liked that description because it puts the emphasis on turning or coiling.

I like to think of the golf swing like a coil spring. On the backswing, you are winding up the spring and storing the power that will be released at impact. I like to break this image down into three parts: coiling, pausing and uncoiling. As I've said earlier, I want all the parts of my swing working in unison. My hips and shoulders coil and uncoil at the same steady pace—a pace matched by my weight shifting back and forward.

I truly believe that one reason my swing has held up as well as it has over the years is that I work very hard on making a good full turn on the backswing. A fellow who has a short swing to begin with is going to lose distance by the ton as he gets on in years, while the player who works at keeping his swing long and fluid will be able to keep up with the youngsters off the tee for quite a number of years.

The player with a good full turn and long swing has one other edge going for him, and it's something I haven't heard many people talk about over the years. I've always felt that because my swing was so long and my tempo was so smooth, I had a chance to save the occasional "off-color" swing. By that I mean that occasionally I'd feel myself out of position—maybe I was slightly off balance or my timing was a bit quick. I was able to make a last-second compensation and save the shot. A fellow with a short swing, say like Doug Sanders or Dan Pohl on the regular tour, might not have time to do that.

Address the Ball in "Halves"   Many people have a tough time figuring out just how they should stand when they address the ball,

Remember the three parts to an effective swing: coil, pause, uncoil. And make them work together.

2

3

4

5

6

7

8

9

10

11

12

13

but the truth is that if you've ever played many sports, the address position is very similar to a ready position in many other sports.

If you think about a basketball player on defense and an outfielder in baseball, you'll notice that they have their weight evenly distributed, their knees are slightly bent, but their backs are straight. If they relaxed their arms, they would dangle loosely, their fingers pointed at their toes.

Perhaps a better example would be a person standing at the side of a pool, ready to dive in. We've all had that experience, but we never think very much about how we go about doing it. Our bodies just react naturally, which is something most of us never give them a chance to do in the golf swing.

I like to stress to people that they think about two keys at address: First, flex your knees comfortably, just as you would to dive into a pool, and keep your legs flexed to the same degree throughout the swing—you want to avoid bobbing up and down because that requires making too many compensations. More often than not, I see people try to play stiff-legged, and that leads to swaying during the swing because your legs are in no position to absorb the weight and motion of your swing.

Second, I tell people to bend slightly at the waist, as though they were forming a "K" with their body. Bending from the waist in this manner allows your shoulders to make the proper turn naturally, which mirrors the path your arms and club are swinging on.

Swing Around Your Head   I imagine that everyone who has ever played this game has heard the saying, "Keep your head down." I also imagine that it's done more people more harm than almost any other piece of advice because it leads people to making very short, restricted swings.

In truth, my head moves during my swing. I turn it slightly to the right as I begin my backswing, and it naturally swivels back to the left on the downswing. Notice, however, that I used the words "turn" and "swivel." What I try to avoid is moving my neck from side to side.

I like to think of my head and neck as the center of my swing, much the same way an axle is the center of a tire's rotation. An axle can turn all it wants, and you'll still get a smooth ride. But if that axle starts moving from side to side, you could be in for a long day—and the same is true with your golf swing.

Let Your Left Arm Be Your Guide   While I'm on the subject of familiar advice, I bet you all "keep your left arm straight." As a result, you see a lot of weekend players get up to hit the ball with their left arm as straight and hard as a two-by-four. Why, they're lucky if they can hit the ball out of their shadow.

Earlier in this section on my keys, I suggested you feel you are pushing the club away from the ball at the start of the swing. This will help you get your swing off to a smooth start, but it also lets your left arm establish the radius, or width, of your swing. The more your left arm bends, the smaller the radius of your swing and the less clubhead speed you'll be able to generate.

Rather than worrying about keeping your left arm straight on the backswing and through impact, I'd rather have you try to address the ball so you could draw a straight line from your left shoulder, down your left arm and the club, to the ball. As you push the clubhead away from the ball with your left hand and arm, try to maintain the feeling of your upper left arm staying in contact with your upper body. This will further help you slow down your swing, and it will also help you make a good turn with your upper body. The combination of the two will go a long way toward keeping your left arm as straight as it needs to be—without your spending a lot of time or energy worrying about it.

Turn Your Hips and Shoulders Together   In a lot of ways a golf swing is like a football team. Everything has to work together to pull off a successful play, but not everyone moves at the same speed or the same distance. Think of a swing as an end sweep, and the clubhead as the runner with the ball.

In order for the play to click, the runner has the farthest distance to travel, so he has to move the fastest. But if he gets out ahead of his blockers, he's in trouble. On the other hand, if his blockers get to their men before he gets to the hole, he's not much better off.

In this comparison, I'd say the hips and shoulders are the blockers. They control the motion of the big muscles, but the distance and the speed they actually move are not nearly the same as those of the runner—or clubhead—or his blocking backs, which would be the arms in the swing.

Relating all this back to my golf swing, I concentrate very heavily on timing and pace, and I've found over the years that if I try to turn my shoulders and hips together, as a team, it helps me swing with a nice tempo. It's when one part of the team gets out of whack that I get into trouble.

I think this advice is especially important for older players. It's just natural to ease up on your turn as you get older because your body isn't as flexible as it once was. As a result, you have a tendency to stop turning and, instead, try to generate clubhead speed by swinging almost entirely with your arms. The problem is, not only does this type of swing not generate power, but because the legs can't support the movement of the swing, you wind up casting the club from the top of your backswing, outside the target line, in an attempt to recover from an awkward and weak position—and the results are the all-too-common banana ball.

I like to think of my knees as the guides to my weight shift. On the backswing, I roll off the inside of my left foot and my left knee reacts by moving to the right. I actually think of it as pointing to the right of the ball. On the downswing, as my weight moves back to the left, my right knee mirrors the action of my left knee. I think that is a pretty good image for you to take to the practice tee: left knee to the right on the backswing, right knee to the left on the downswing—and keep both of those knees flexed throughout the swing.

Don't Forget Your Feet   Golf is a game that is played from the ground up. If you don't have a good solid base to play from, the force of the swing will throw you off balance and your chances of making consistently solid contact are reduced dramatically.

But almost as important is my belief that proper footwork can control the pace of your swing. People spend so much time worrying about things like the swing plane that they overlook the importance of footwork in making a good swing. But footwork is every bit as important in golf as it is in any other sport—and maybe a little bit more important.

In my case, when I feel my swing getting a little off-color, the first thing I check is my footwork. The key to a good swing is timing, and timing begins from the ground up.

Now some people say that you ought to have most of your weight set toward your toes, since that will prevent you from losing your balance on your backswing. Still others teach that the weight should be back on your heels, since that helps prevent you from falling forward on the downswing. Well, common sense tells me that if enough people disagree on something like this, the best answer is probably a compromise, and that's the case here. I like to feel that my weight is evenly balanced between my toes and heels. And as I mentioned a little earlier, I like to pinch my knees together slightly to help maintain the sensation of playing from the insides of my feet. I want to feel centered during the swing as much as possible. I want to avoid getting my weight to the outside of my feet, especially my right foot on the backswing, at all costs.

At address, I like to toe out my feet slightly, since I think this gives me a better base to play from. But you don't want to overdo this. If your toes point out too much, you'll severely restrict your ability to make a good turn and weight shift.

Another point of debate among teaching pros and top players is when and how much the heels of your feet should come off the ground during the swing. Again, some people teach that the left heel should remain anchored to the ground during the swing, since this gives you a better chance at a consistent swing. By lifting the heel on the backswing and replacing it at the start of the downswing, they argue that you leave yourself open to spinning your hips out to the left prematurely if your heel doesn't return to its original position.

Now there's a certain amount of truth to that if you are young, flexible or playing short to medium irons where there isn't as much weight shift. However, most people instinctively raise their left heel as the motion and weight of their swing moves to the right side on the backswing. This becomes increasingly true as the clubs become longer. By trying to arbitrarily anchor your left foot, most people will run the risk of hanging their weight back on the left side on the backswing rather than making the full, fluid weight shift we've talked about so often.

The action of the right heel is a little more complicated. You can take it for a fact that it will rise off the turf on the downswing. The force and motion of the swing will see to that. What you need to guard against is releasing your right heel too quickly in the swing. In truth, that's more of an indication that your hips have cleared to the left a little too quickly in the swing, and since something has to give, it causes your heel to come off the ground well before the ball is struck.

I realize that trying to explain something like the action of your heels during the swing may strike some of you as pretty cosmic stuff, and I'm inclined to agree. But I'm doing this to make a point. Footwork is crucial to the success of your swing, and it is too often overlooked. Just try to remember what I've said before: At impact, you want to try to be in roughly the same position you were in at address. The closer you can come to doing that, the better off you'll be.

While I'm on the subject of footwork, I'd like to relate a story that I think may help you.

For most of my career I was managed by a wonderful Boston Irishman named Fred Corcoran. Fred was a dear friend and I owe him a lot. He was a genius at getting my name in the papers, and one time at the Masters he came up with a scheme that was a beauty—and got me into a little hot water.

Fred played up my so-called hillbilly upbringing to the hilt. I had mentioned to him that I learned to play golf in my bare feet, and that the game never got complicated for me until someone gave me my first pair of golf shoes. Well, that was pretty much the truth. As a kid we'd go barefoot all through the summer and a good part of the spring and fall to boot. In fact, I told Fred that when my swing started to go sour, I liked to sneak off, take off my shoes and just practice barefooted. It gave me a better sense of feel and it improved my timing because, without those spikes to anchor me, I had to slow my swing down or I'd be falling all over the lot.

Well, we got to Augusta National, which has always been what you'd call a pretty staid place, and Fred got talking to the press guys, who were all old pals of his. He told them that if they thought I was good with shoes on, they ought to see what I could do to the old girl in my bare feet. Next thing you know I was out on the course, with that beautiful green grass coming up through my toes and what seemed like every writer in the place by my side for a practice round. It felt so natural that I turned in one of my best rounds ever.

The writers had a field day. Fred was in heaven, and I was happy to get the publicity. Unfortunately, not everyone was as thrilled. Gene Sarazen tore into me, both in person and in the papers, for pulling off what he called a "publicity stunt." I was sorry he felt that way, but I figured I wasn't hurting anyone and it was good publicity for the tournament. Besides, as Jimmy Demaret told Gene, if it wasn't for publicity stunts, he "might still be on a banana boat on his way over from the old country."

Anyway, if there was one thing I regretted in the whole business, it was that people took it as kind of a lark, and didn't get the message that kicking off those shoes and practicing barefoot can do a world of good for your swing. If you're too self-conscious to get down to what Mother Nature gave you, try hitting balls in sneakers. It's not as good, but it's not bad.

My Keys to Better Timing

I've been blessed in a number of ways throughout my career. I was always a pretty good athlete. I just naturally enjoy competing and the pressure that comes from being in contention. And my body has held up pretty well over the years—although if the Devil himself came along and offered me one more good year without my eye problems, my back problems and a few other aches and pains, I do believe I might be sorely tempted to listen to his offer.

But as I look back over the years, I think that the biggest reason my swing has held up as well as it has is that I've always concentrated very hard on my rhythm and timing. I've tried to stress this in earlier sections, but I think it's so important that I want to repeat it a few times, just to make sure it sinks in. You can have the best mechanics in the world, but if your timing is off, sooner or later your swing is going to let you down—and that's especially true when you are under pressure, which naturally makes your timing speed up.

Notice that I mentioned both rhythm and timing. Rhythm is the speed that you swing, and timing is the coordination between all the different elements of the swing. The reason I stress the importance of rhythm is that a fast swing doesn't allow you as much room for error as you try to fit all the parts of the swing together. A slower, more graceful rhythm is a lot easier to control.

For what it's worth, I may have played in more pro-am events than anyone else alive. And it's a safe bet that I've studied more amateurs over a $5 nassau than you could shake a stick at. After all these years I totally agree with the old saying that there's no prettier sight on the first tee than an opponent with a fast backswing and a fat wallet—the faster and fatter the better.

Think about your own game. Which club do you have more confidence in, a driver, 5-iron or 8-iron? If you're like most people, it's probably an 8-iron. Now that's partially because it has the shortest shaft and is easier to control, but I believe a more important reason is that most folks take the club for what it is and don't try to kill the ball. They make a smooth, comfortable swing and, most times, get pretty fair results.

On the other hand, put a driver in someone's hands and there's no telling where the ball is going to wind up. Why? Because people haul back and swing out of their shoes, trying to hit the ball just as hard as they can. The truth is, there's been damn few people who can let out the shaft that way with much success, and if you're honest with yourself, I think you'll find that you've never had much success when you've tried to pound the ball to smithereens.

Swing Under Control   By the time I came out on the tour, Bob Jones had already retired from competitive golf, but I did get to know him from playing in the Masters and, of course, I heard a lot of stories about him from the other players.

One trick he had that might help the average golfer was taking one more club than he needed when he was under pressure. In other words, if he had what would normally be a 6-iron shot, he'd pull a 5-iron and just focus on making a smooth swing. He knew that, under stress, there is always a temptation to speed up your swing, and that was his way of guarding against it.

I've always tried to swing at about 85 percent of my top speed. That's a pace I can control, and by swinging a little slower and smoother, if I do miss the shot, at least I have a fighting chance of recovering and saving par. If I haul off and try to powder the ball, I might hit the shot off the world, and it doesn't take too many mistakes like that to send you down the road.

A lot of people who have had problems with the timing of their swing have been successful if they just imagine that, no matter what club they have in their hands, they are swinging a club they are comfortable with—usually a short iron. If you're a player whose swing gets a little quick at times (and be honest with yourself), then it might be worth your while to go to a practice tee, hit a dozen or so shots with your favorite club and gradually work up through the longer clubs, trying very hard to make the same full swing with the same good tempo.

Follow "Doc's" Example   Dr. Cary Middlecoff was one of the top players in the late 1940s and throughout the '50s. In his prime, Doc attracted a lot of attention because he actually paused at the top of his backswing. Now that takes a lot of talent and strength, but I do think it's a good mental image to have, even if you might not be strong enough to actually do it.

As I said earlier, I like to think of my swing as a coil spring that winds up its power on the backswing and then releases it on the downswing. I take it one step further by feeling that I pause at the top of my backswing. I may not pause quite the way Doc did, but by thinking about it, I do two things that I think are important: First, I set up a key to a slow, steady backswing, and second, I make sure that I complete my backswing rather than cutting my swing off and lunging at the ball.

Finally, one last thought while I've been talking about my "coil spring" analogy: If you were going to wind a spring and then release it, the coils of the spring would move the same way, back and forth. I try to imagine my swing moving in the same manner. As I've mentioned, one of my most important keys is returning my body and the club to the same position at impact that it was in at address. To do that, it makes sense for me to try to return the clubhead to the ball on the same path that I took it away on the backswing. Actually, the paths may vary slightly, but in this case it's the idea that counts—and I think it's an idea that will work for you.

Summing Up

As I said at the start of this chapter, my keys are ones that I've developed over the years. They've worked for me, but they might not all work for you. Everyone is different, and if the golf swing was something you could walk into the drugstore and buy, there'd be a hell of a lot more good players around.

The truth is that finding the right keys for yourself takes a lot of trial and error. I suggest keeping a small notebook in your bag, and when you find something that works, jot it down and refer back to it when your swing isn't working. I've found that I tend to fall back on the same mistakes, and with experience I know what keys to try to correct those mistakes. If you are honest with yourself when you review your own game, I bet you'll find that the same weaknesses tend to crop up in your game. Finding the keys to correct those problems should be your first order of business.

I want to go back and stress one other point that I made earlier in this section. I've given you a lot of keys to pick and choose from, but remember that to make these keys pay off, you can focus on only one or two at a time. Trying to accommodate any more than that is useless and counterproductive. And finally, the time to find out what key or keys are likely to work best for you is before your round, as you warm up. If a key had paid off in your last round, go back to it.

Often a single key will get you through several rounds before it goes stale and you have to search and find another. But as long as you have another to fall back on, you should be able to get through the round—then head for the practice tee and find a key that will work for you the next time out.

The Game Explodes
The 1950s and 1960s

*P*rofessional golf really took off in this era. People had a little extra money and time, President Eisenhower and, to a lesser degree, President Kennedy were avid golfers, and television brought the game into millions of homes. More and more golfers became household names, and more and more money went into purses. I'm not sure that the golfers got any better, but there were more good ones to beat. The same is true today, only more so. Here are my recollections of some of the best from this era.

Raymond Floyd Unlike a lot of players from this era, Raymond did not come on tour on the heels of a great amateur career. Hell, I'm not sure he ever was really an amateur. He turned pro at age nineteen and joined the tour two years later, winning a tournament his first year out.

Raymond has a lot of ability, but his greatest strength may be that he is a fearless competitor. There's just no backdown in that boy. He'll go at you all day long.

I remember when he first came out on tour, he arranged to get into a practice round with me and Johnny Farrell's son, Billy, who has been a fine player for a long time. We were at Greensboro, where I had won eight times. You might say I had a pretty good feel for the course.

I got off to a bad start, and was in the hole to both Raymond and Billy at the turn. I offered to double the bets on the back. Billy had seen that act before and said no. Raymond wanted all of me he could get, which is what he got. I shot a 28 on the back and that was that.

Even though I got him, Raymond showed me a lot that day. He had a lot of belief in his ability and wasn't afraid to back it up. It didn't surprise me that he's gone on to become one of the top players.

People make a lot of the fact that Raymond isn't afraid to play for a little something during practice rounds, but they forget that when he came up, that was what most of us did. You'd play for enough to keep your attention and sharpen your game, but not enough so that it would get nasty out there. I think it helped Raymond. I know it helped me.

Doc Middlecoff   Doc is another one of those players who kind of get lost in the shuffle, and folks forget just how good he really was. He didn't play that long, from 1947 to 1961, but he won thirty-three tournaments, including two U.S. Opens and a Masters. That's a pretty impressive record in any era.

Doc was one of the better tall players I ever saw. He could really bust the ball and he was an audacious putter. He was eventually done in by a bad back, but I think he would have had a pretty short career either way because he was so high-strung. In fact, I'd say that of all the really good players I've known, Doc was easily the most nervous.

If he'd had just a little of Jimmy Demaret's temperament, there's no telling what might have been.

Jack Nicklaus Jack would be right near the top of anyone's list of great players. He's won more major championships and been leading money winner often enough to earn his rightful place in history, and I think that's what Jack was always playing for—history.

Unlike many players who came from what you'd call modest backgrounds, Jack came from a family that was very comfortable, so money was never a driving concern. Contrast that with Ben or Byron or even Arnold Palmer, and that gave Jack, if not an edge, at least a slightly different outlook. He never wore himself out playing a lot of events or doing a lot of outings. In my era, you made your living from outings and exhibitions, not from purses. By the time Jack came along, that had changed.

I don't think Jack was the best shotmaker among the top players, but if you needed a guy to hit a tough shot with everything on the line, Jack could pull it off. He had that much confidence and that much ability to concentrate. He actually enjoys feeling the pressure of being in contention. It's fun for him. It's hell for a lot of other players.

Jack was an exceptional driver and long iron player, but he was never much of a threat with a wedge in his hand, either from the bunkers or around the greens. Lee Trevino once said that if Jack had a wedge, everyone else could go home. That's pretty strong, but not too far off the mark. He was our best putter for a long, long time. He'd kill you with the blade, saving five or six shots a round.

I'd put Jack up there with Ben and Bobby Locke for having the most self-control. If he made a bogie, you could see the red rise up his neck and he'd walk a little slower to give himself some time to cool off, but I never saw him hit two bad shots in a row. Jack never beat himself.

Jack was always very considerate of his fellow players, and I enjoyed playing with him. People complained about his slow play, but he actually moved along pretty well. He was deliberate over a shot, but he raced along between shots. If you weren't careful, he'd walk you to death.

People often ask if I think Jack will have a big impact on the Senior Tour. I doubt it, mostly because I don't think he'll play that much. He doesn't have anything to prove, to himself or anyone else. His place in history is secure.

Arnold Palmer   Arnold is a perfect example of the old saying, "You live by the putter and you die by the putter." In his prime, he was as good a putter as you'd ever see. He'd hit the ball all over the lot, get it on the green and bang it into the hole. He was extremely aggressive, and never worried for a second about the 3-footer he might have coming back. But when his putting left him, it left him stone cold. I imagine he's tried thousands of putters and techniques over the years, hoping to rediscover the magic. The problem is, the magic in putting is confidence, and that's a very fragile commodity.

Of course, Arnold's struggles have just made him that much more popular with the fans. They can honestly relate and sympathize with him, just as they have throughout his career. I remember that when he quit smoking it was front-page news, which is how it should be, because Arnold always loved the galleries and got a lot of strength from their support.

If the truth be known, Arnold may be a better ball striker today than in previous years. He's a better driver, and he doesn't hit as many of those wild hooking darters anymore. In the old days, the combination of a strong grip and a closed clubface could get him in all sorts of trouble.

Even so, he had a world of guts and he'd hitch up his slacks and give it a rip. It may not always have been pretty, but it always was exciting and it sure was good for the game.

Gary Player   I would say that Gary, based on his record, got more out of his game than anyone else I know. If someone had bet me that back in 1957, when he first came out on tour, Gary would win as many tournaments as he has, and played so well for so long, that person could have taken me for the farm.

I think Gary's devotion to physical fitness gave him a big edge.

He never smoked or drank or partied around, and he was careful to pace himself so he avoided being burned out. The key to playing well for the long haul is taking enough time away from the tour to recharge your batteries, and the fact that Gary went back and forth to his home in South Africa may have actually helped him in that sense.

Lately, Gary has been somewhat controversial because he's been claiming that his wins in the so-called Senior Majors should count alongside his wins in the U.S. and British Opens, the PGA and the Masters.

In all honesty, I don't think they should count, any more than I think the Players Championship should count. The Majors exist as a measure of accomplishment from one era to the next. For that matter, if you want to count Majors, we counted some other tournaments as Majors when I first came up. If you won the Los Angeles Open, the Metropolitan Open, the Western or the North and South, you had beaten the top fields and earned yourself a bonus from the equipment manufacturers. When you come right down to it, I never understood why the Canadian Open never counted as a Major. After all, Canada is a pretty good-sized country.

Peter Thomson   When Peter first came here from Australia, he didn't look as if he'd do much. But looks are deceiving, as he proved by winning five British Opens and nine tournaments on the Senior Tour in 1985.

Peter has one of the best dispositions for this game that I've ever seen. He's very bright and totally unflappable. He's got a very solid short game and has always been a good putter. His swing is compact and very simple, and holds up well under pressure. On top of that, he's sneaky long because he makes such solid contact. The only mystery to me is why he ran for Parliament back home in Australia. Why spend your time arguing with politicians when you could be fishing or playing golf?

Lee Trevino   Lee Trevino didn't even come out on tour until he was twenty-eight, which makes his record even all the more remarkable. Lee is one of the best shotmakers I've ever seen, and is also totally fearless. When it comes to most players, not only do they know he can beat them, but they also know that he knows he can beat them. That gives Lee a tremendous edge going into a final round.

When he first came out, people criticized his swing, but he keeps the clubhead on line for a long time, he doesn't have to worry about a hook, and it works for him, day in and day out.

People talk about natural players, and Lee falls into that category. But what people don't understand is how hard even naturals have to work at this game. When Lee came out, he had a tough time playing bunker shots because he rarely faced one growing up in Texas. Not only did he learn how to play from bunkers, he also became one of the best in the business.

Shotmaking
The Fun Begins

*F*or me, the greatest fun in this game is being able to hit the shots that are required—fade or draw, high shot or low—when the pressure is on. Over the years many players have established fine records, but much of their success was due to their ability to drain putts from off the earth or to salvage pars with chipping and pitching. I say more power to them, but for me, the players I've always admired were the guys who could paint masterpieces with a club and a ball.

In the previous sections we've gone over the fundamentals of the swing, and like anything else, you need to walk before you can run. But if you're comfortable with your walking, so to speak, let's pick up the pace and get to the part of the game that separates the men from the boys.

The Big Money Era (1970s–1980s)

Top: Johnny Miller, Chip Beck, Payne Stewart, Fred Couples
Middle: Paul Azinger, Bob Tway, Fuzzy Zoeller, Lanny Wadkins
Bottom: Curtis Strange, Hal Sutton, Ben Crenshaw, Tom Watson

Memorable Tournaments

Top: Ben Hogan, 1953; Ralph Guldahl, 1937
Bottom: Byron Nelson, 1939; Lew Worsham, 1947

The Rules of the Road

Without getting overly technical, a few basics govern how a ball will react when it's hit: clubface position at impact, clubhead speed and swing path. By altering these three factors, you apply the necessary spin to the ball to make it curve and to determine whether it flies higher or lower than normal.

For example, if the clubface is open when it strikes the ball, and it comes into the ball from either straight down the target line or from slightly outside-to-inside the target line, the ball will have a clockwise spin and will fade from left to right. The greater the clubhead speed, or the more open the clubface at impact, the greater the spin, and that nice little fade grows into a slice.

On the other hand, if a clubface is closed at impact, and the club strikes the ball from either down the target line or from inside the line, the ball will have a counterclockwise spin and will draw from right to left—with a severe spin producing a hook.

As a general rule, a ball that is hit with a fade or slice spin will fly higher and roll less than a ball with hook spin.

In this section I'll go over in more detail the mechanics of hitting these shots, but first I want to make a general statement about shotmaking. There's a school of thought that teaches people to alter their grip to hit different shots. For example, turning your hands slightly to the left allows your wrists to release more quickly, which, in turn, allows the clubface to close down on impact, producing a draw or hook. By weakening your grip—or setting the hands slightly more to the left—the clubhead releases later, the clubface is open at impact, and the result is a fade or slice.

In an extreme situation I might alter my grip ever so slightly, but in most cases I'd advise against it. If you have a good grip, it will allow you to manipulate the ball simply by altering your stance, which, in turn, changes the clubhead's path into the ball, producing the desired spin. It's a lot simpler and safer method. A good grip is difficult to develop, and I'd avoid doing anything to tamper with it.

Hitting a Draw

You may have heard the statement "All good players fight a hook." To a large degree that's true because a good swing delivers the clubhead to the ball from inside the target line to a point where, at impact, it is square to the ball. The result is either a straight ball or a ball that curves ever so slightly to the left. When a good swing gets out of kilter, however, most times that nice little draw turns into a raging hook, which is what that statement means. The player with a weak swing would give his or her right arm to be able to get into a position to hook the ball. In that sense, this particular section might be particularly helpful. It's like the old story about the amateur who asked Tommy Bolt how to cure his slice.

"Get a hook," said Tommy.

For most people, when they want to hit a straight shot, they address the ball with their feet parallel to the target line. Everything else being equal, this allows them to deliver the clubhead from right down the target line.

To draw or hook the ball, the clubface either has to be closed slightly at address or has to come into the ball from inside the target line and be closing down at impact. The best way to do this is to close your stance, pulling your right foot back away from the target line while moving your left foot slightly closer to the line. The more your stance is closed, the more the clubhead can be delivered from inside the target line and the more the ball will curve from right to left.

I like to give people this analogy for hitting this type of shot. If you wanted to skip a flat rock across a pond, you'd want that rock coming into the water at the flattest possible angle, and to do this you'd need to swing your arm just the same way you need to swing the club to draw the ball—from inside your target line.

Now think about how you stride when you want to skip a stone. Does your left foot move to the left—opening your stance—or does it move straight forward or does it stride to the right? If you think about it, I think you'll find that it moves to the right, allowing your throwing arm to whip around your body. It's the same principle when you want to draw or hook the ball.

Here's a tip that I think might help you get the feel for hitting the ball from inside the target line: The next time you're practicing, place a ball down with the trademark or stripe pointing right at the target. Now, to draw the ball, turn the stripe slightly so that, if it were a clockface, the small hand would point to the seven. To get the feel for hitting the ball from inside the line, simply try to strike the ball right on the stripe. Conversely, if you want to put the opposite spin on the ball, simply move the stripe so it would point to the five on the clubface. In trying to hit the stripe you'll be forced to strike the ball from an outside-to-in swing path, and the ball should curve to the right. This is also a good tip when you're teeing the ball, especially on par 3s.

Hitting a ball with a right-to-left spin is a stronger shot because it tends to give the ball overspin. The good news is that this is a good shot to hit when you're trying to scratch out a little more distance. The bad news is that it won't stop as quickly, so if the shot is off line, you run the risk of its bouncing into trouble more readily than a straight ball or a ball hit with a fade.

Hitting a Fade

Over the years a fade has been the bread-and-butter shot for a lot of good players. Where Bobby Jones liked to draw the ball, players like Jack Nicklaus, Lee Trevino and Ben Hogan have elevated the fade into an art form.

As I mentioned at the close of the last section, a fade is a good shot for accuracy because it will check up quicker than a draw, partially because it flies a little higher and lands a little softer.

The address position for a fade is just the opposite from the position you're in to draw the ball. Since you want to come into the ball from outside the line with a slightly open clubface, it makes sense that you'd draw your left foot back off the target line. It is also helpful to play the ball slightly forward in your stance. This requires some experimentation, but try playing it off your left heel and see what happens.

To return to my analogy of throwing a rock, suppose you wanted to toss a rock over a tall tree or building. How would you stand? I hope that, after you've thought about it, you find that you'd pull your left foot back, which helps get your hips out of the way and allows your right arm to make a motion similar to the one required to hit a fade.

A couple of final thoughts on fading and drawing the ball: When you want to draw the ball, a good thought to keep in mind is that your hands and wrists should be especially relaxed. I like the term "oily." You want your hands to release freely through the hitting area, allowing the toe of the club to turn over the ball. On the other hand, to fade the ball you want the clubface to remain open at impact. My thought for this shot is to hold on a little tighter with my left hand. I don't let my left wrist break or release until after the ball has been struck.

Finally, when you are making your club selection to play either a fade or a draw, you should keep in mind that a draw is a stronger shot, while a fade is a weaker one. It's a subtle consideration, but subtlety is what saves strokes down the stretch.

Hitting the High Shot

Being able to control the trajectory of your shots comes in handy when you are playing in adverse weather conditions, are trying to escape from trouble or need to fit a shot to a difficult pin position.

Much in golf is common sense, and that's true when it comes to hitting high or low shots. If you follow the basic guidelines I'm about to give you, and take the time to practice, you'll be able to add a whole new dimension to your golf game.

To hit the ball high, you need to be able to add loft to the club. In many respects, the mechanics are similar to those of fading the ball. Essentially, what you are trying to do is strike the ball with a more sharply descending blow than you would for a normal shot. You do this by altering both your address position and the path of your swing.

I recommend opening your stance slightly and playing the ball forward in your stance. In fact, a good rule of thumb is that your hands should be behind the ball at address when you want to hit a high shot, and they should be ahead of the ball when you want to play a low shot.

To hit a high shot, I want to make a more V-shaped swing than normal, and to do this I take the clubhead away from the ball with a quick break of the wrist. I also take the club away on an outside swing path, which will further add loft to the club. My final swing thought for this shot is to make a nice high finish. It might help if you keep this saying in mind: Reach for the sky to hit the ball high.

Hitting the Low Shot

Being able to hit the ball low is a particularly good skill to have, since it will be invaluable when playing in a strong wind or when trying to escape from trouble.

In truth, this is a lot easier shot for the average player than the shot you need to hit the ball high. It's a shorter, more compact swing that allows you to trap the ball and send it scampering.

Play the ball back in your stance, in the middle of your stance or maybe even slightly farther back than that. You'll have to experiment and see what works best for you. Set your hands ahead of the ball, since that is the position you'll want them in at impact. Set your weight on your left side and keep it there throughout the swing. There is virtually no weight shift on this shot.

As I mentioned before, this is a short swing. You need to take the club back only far enough so that your hands are about shoulder high. From this position, drive down on the ball without breaking your wrists. There's not much follow-through on this shot—all you are doing is punching down on the ball.

One final bit of advice on this shot: Too often I see people trying to hit low shots by hitting down with a very hard swing. The result is a ball that balloons up into the air. To avoid this, think "solid" contact, not "hard" contact. One other reminder: With this shot, you are effectively taking loft off the club, thus making a 7-iron play with a 6-iron or 5-iron loft. For that reason, I suggest you never try this shot with anything less than a 5-iron, since otherwise you run the risk of driving the ball down onto the turf because you've taken all the loft off the iron.

Reading the Situation

Before you can become an effective shotmaker, you need to be able to understand how course conditions will affect the shot you are trying to play. There will be times when the shot you need and want to hit will be impossible to play because of one of these three factors: the lie, the wind and the changes in elevation.

Of the three, the lie is the most important because it is the first consideration you must make. If you have a bad lie, you have to take your medicine and write it off as the rub of the green. Let me run through some basic types of lies you might face and give you some tips on how to play from them.

Uphill   If you have a lie where your left or front foot is above your right foot, the tendency is for the ball to draw to the left and run a bit farther than it would for the normal shot. The lie will also cause the club to reach the bottom of the swing earlier than it would on a level lie, so I suggest moving the ball back in your stance. Depending on the severity of the slope, you need to guard against too much weight shifting to the right on the backswing. I suggest anchoring most of your weight on your left side, avoiding much of a weight shift. You need stability from these awkward lies. A good rule of thumb for these shots is to align your shoulders to the slope of the lie and then try to swing the clubhead along a path that mirrors the slope of the lie as much as possible. In doing this, you give yourself a slightly greater margin for error.

Downhill   This is a much more difficult shot than one from an uphill lie. You want to play the ball slightly forward in your stance,

Remember—the way you approach your shot is determined by the lie and any changes in elevation. Of the two, the lie is always the most important.

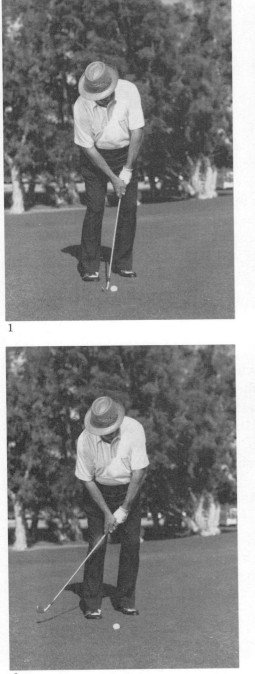

1

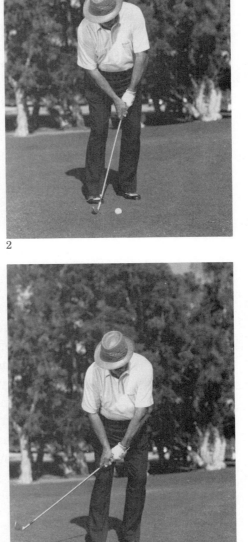

2

3

4

5

6

7

8

with your weight braced on your right side, which will help fight the tendency to fall to the left during the swing. The ball will fly to the right from this lie, and it won't be as strong a shot as one from an uphill lie, so make sure you take plenty of club.

Ball Below Your Feet   The trouble with this shot is that the ball will fly to the right from this lie, so you must allow for this in planning your shot. The danger in this shot is that the motion of the swing makes it very easy for your weight to get out over your toes, pulling you forward. You must give yourself a good base to play from, and that means you should address the ball with most of your weight set back on your heels. It is also very important to flex your knees and keep them flexed throughout the swing, since this will help keep your swing in balance and help you resist the temptation to rise up out of the shot prematurely.

Ball Above Your Feet   This lie dictates that the ball will fly to the left, and the more severe the lie, the more it will do so. While it does complicate the shot, unless the lie is very severe, it is not quite as difficult a shot as one where the ball is well below your feet, if only because you can make a much more stable swing. Your weight will be out over your toes, and you should play the ball back slightly in your stance. The key thought on this type of shot is to try to restrict your release. Since the ball wants to go to the left, if you can hit a hold shot and keep the clubhead moving to the target, you can hit a straighter shot. Like any of these shots, however, it takes a lot of practice to hit these with confidence in competition.

The Flier   When you find your ball in the rough, or if you have a lie in the fairway with grass between the ball and the clubhead, you run the risk of catching a flier. It's similar to a spitball in baseball. The moisture in the grass takes much of the backspin off the ball, and as a result, it flies farther than a normal shot and will run farther once it lands. The answer to this problem is to take one less club and allow for the added carry and roll. You also must be realistic and realize that the ball is not going to check up on the green the way a shot struck cleanly will.

Having said all that, this is where all the controversy over irons with square grooves comes into play. Clubs with square grooves virtually eliminate fliers, especially if you are playing a wound balata ball. The configuration and spacing of the grooves negate the effects of the flier lie and allow players to spin the ball out of lies they hadn't been able to stop a shot from before.

I don't like square grooves for two reasons. First, I think they take the edge away from the accurate player who has learned to avoid the rough. In that sense, you're penalizing the wrong guy. Second, when the clubs are new and the grooves are fresh, they tend to "balloon" the ball into the air, especially in a head wind. This costs as much as a half a club in distance, which is a pretty big trade-off.

Dealing with the Wind

I've always felt that playing in the wind was one way to separate the men from the boys when it comes to shotmaking. If you can control the ball, you have a much better chance of posting a good score when the winds start to gust and howl.

Actually, I've always liked playing in a little wind because it gives you something to bank the ball into. I think that a confident shotmaker, given the choice, will always try to work the ball into the wind rather than simply hanging the ball out into the wind and letting it drift back to the target. It's simply a stronger and more reliable shot.

The key to playing in the wind is making solid contact as often as possible. Weak, mishit shots are particularly vulnerable, so I would stress playing the shots you feel most comfortable with.

One other piece of advice on the wind: An approach shot hit into the wind will have a better chance of checking on the green because the wind will actually increase the backspin on the ball. However, the opposite is true of a shot played downwind. You can stand there all day, and unless the greens are very soft or slope toward you, that ball is not going to check up.

How much a head or tail wind will affect your shot depends on how strong a player you are, but as a rule of thumb I think you can figure that it's a club difference for each 10 miles per hour of wind. Therefore, if you've got a 20 mile-per-hour wind in your face, and you're facing what is normally a 7-iron shot, you'd better drop down to a 5-iron. And remember, the harder you hit the ball, the more it will balloon up into the wind, so in a head wind, if you are between clubs, always take one more club and swing easily.

Finally, one last thing to remember about the wind: The more humid and heavy the air, the more the wind will affect your shot. It took me a while to figure that out, but once I did it gave me a tremendous edge over the other fellows when the tour swung through Florida.

The Highs and Lows

One of the toughest lessons to get a feel for is how much changes in elevation will affect a shot. In fact, one of the most frequently overlooked elements at Augusta National is how dramatically the elevation changes on those holes. When people talk about the value of experience in playing the Masters, this is one of the areas they are talking about.

If you are hitting an approach shot to an elevated green, you must take more club, and of course, the opposite is true when playing the green below you. Also, a ball hit to an elevated green will not check up as quickly as a ball hit to a green below you. The reason is that a ball hit to an elevated green will reach the green on a flatter trajectory.

Know Your Yardages

In this section I'm really talking about two subjects in one. The first is the importance of knowing exactly how far you have to your target and the second—and probably more important—is why knowing how far you hit each club is crucial to any hopes of success you might have.

When I was learning to play, people played by eyesight alone. Until recently, there were no yardage books telling you how far you were from the green, or sprinkler heads marked off with the yardage, or even 150-yard markers that are on most courses today. You simply studied the shot, and you judged by experience which club you needed for the shot at hand. Obviously, this required some trial and error, and it was easy to be fooled by swales in the fairway short of the green, or by subtle changes in elevation.

I guess the first good player who began using yardage notes was Deane Beman, who is now the commissioner of the PGA Tour but who was an outstanding amateur before turning pro. He convinced Jack Nicklaus that it was a good idea, and once the word got around that Jack was doing it, well, everyone followed suit.

The biggest advantage to playing strictly by yardage is that it removes one element of doubt from your mind. Certainly, as we just discussed, there are other considerations—the wind, the lie and the changes in elevation—but by knowing the exact yardage, you have a basis to begin a logical club selection.

Of course, none of this really helps unless you have an accurate knowledge of how far you honestly hit each club. And I can't stress "honestly" enough. If I had to pick one glaring weakness that I've seen in amateurs over the years, it's that they always expect to hit their best shot—their "Sunday punch." As a result, nine times out of ten they come up short of the green. If you don't believe me, then come out to a tour event some Wednesday and watch the pro-am. Find a medium-length par 3 and watch the teams play through. I think—no, I know—what you'll see is the great majority of the amateurs coming up short of the flag while the pros, if they do miss the green, will at least have taken enough club to get them close to pin high.

In my case, the distance between clubs varies roughly 10 yards. In other words, I'm most comfortable hitting a 5-iron from 165 yards. I can hit comfortably as much as 170 yards or as little as 160, but once I get outside those limits, I'll switch clubs. Remember, these figures are based on clear, dry, windless conditions.

How many of you can honestly say that you know your yardages for each club? Not many, I'd bet, and the odds would be on my side. Here's how you can find out.

The best way is to take a dozen new balls, of the type you usually play with—new, because they won't be out of round or have gone stale, and the type you play with, because different kinds of balls react differently. For example, a solid ball will tend to fly farther than a wound ball. Go to your practice range or a nearby field and work your way through your set, beginning with your sand wedge and finishing with the driver. Realistically, this is a long process, so you might want to do it over several sessions. Hit the dozen balls, then pace off the distance to the balls. To do this correctly, you'll have to measure the exact distance of your stride ahead of time to get an accurate measurement of the distance you hit each club.

Once you've reached the balls, discount your longest and shortest balls, and measure only to where the majority of the balls end up. It also helps if the ground is soft, so that you're getting a measurement of how far you carry the ball and not how far it carries and rolls.

As I said, this is the best way to do it, but many of you may not have the time or the access to a range. If not, you'll have to do the best you can to approximate this test. I would, however, warn you against going to a driving range and relying on the distance markers. For one thing, the balls at most ranges are so bad that you won't get an accurate measure of how far you hit the ball, and secondly, the distance markers at most ranges aren't accurate—they move the markers in to soothe people's egos and make them think they hit the ball farther than they really do.

Play to Your Strengths

It is important to be able to work the ball a number of different ways, but when you get under the gun, the key is to go with your bread-and-butter shot. As they say, when you get to the party, it's a good idea to dance with the one who brought you.

I remember being paired with my nephew, J.C., in the 1979 PGA Championship at Oakland Hills, outside Detroit. I've always been partial to that course, and I was playing very well—so well, in fact, that I was hammering par and picking up a lot of support from the fans and the press, who enjoyed seeing old Sam take one more run at the brass ring.

Now J.C. and I have always enjoyed giving each other the needle in a friendly way, but seeing me play as well as I was, he was like a little kid out there, pulling for me every step of the way.

On the second day, as we stood on the 18th tee, he said, "Now, Sam, you're not going to hit that dinky little fade of yours off this tee, are you?"

"Well, I do want to be in the fairway," I said, and that's exactly what I hit and what I did. I wound up making my second straight birdie on the hole, which was especially sweet since it's a killer hole that the members play as a par 5 and we played as a 4. If you look at it that way, I figure I was good for back-to-back eagles.

The point of the story is that rather than gamble under pressure, I stayed with the shot I had been successful with that week—a nice, solid fade—rather than get greedy and gamble on something new.

My advice is to play to your strength—either a fade or draw— under pressure. You'll remove just a trace of doubt from your mind going in, and that may be all it takes to help you pull off the shot you need to hit.

Learning to Concentrate

I'm going to make a pretty strong point here: You can have all the talent and determination in the world, but if you can't concentrate you'll never realize a tenth of your potential.

Tommy Bolt was one of the most talented players I ever saw. He had a great swing and could hit all the shots, but as soon as something went wrong Tommy would fly off the handle. Now I've lost my temper a time or two, and nobody ever got more clubs airborne than Bobby Jones when he was younger, but you have to be able to right yourself and get back to the job at hand. To me, that's concentration, and if Tommy could have learned that, there's no telling how good he could have been.

There's much to admire in Jack Nicklaus's game, but I've always respected him for his ability to concentrate. I've seen Jack miss a shot and you can actually watch the red rise up his neck. You know that inside he's steaming, but he never shows it, and by the time he's reached his ball for his next shot, the only thing he's thinking about is the job at hand.

The key to concentrating properly is playing in the present tense. Don't spend all your energies on something that just happened— either good or bad—and avoid thinking about what lies ahead. There's been a lot of players who had a tournament practically won, only to let it slip away by thinking about the trophy or what they plan to do with the winner's purse. I've always told people, you can't do anything about the past, and you've got to play your way into the future.

When people talk about players who could really concentrate, they invariably mention Ben Hogan. I suppose I know Ben as a player about as well as anyone. It's true that when the starter said, "Gentlemen, play away," Ben would narrow those steely blues of his and go off in a trance.

One year Ben was paired with Claude Harmon at the Masters. He and Claude were good friends, but when Ben went to work on the course he was all business. They came to the 12th hole, which is one of the most difficult par 3s in the world. Birdies are rare, and you could grow old waiting for anyone to make an ace there.

Well, sure enough, Claude came along and made a hole in one. The crowd exploded and roared again a few minutes later when Ben made his putt for a two. As they were walking off the green, Ben said to Claude, "You know, I can't remember the last time I made a birdie there in competition. What'd you make, Claude?"

"Why Ben, I made a hole in one," said Claude, who was dumbfounded.

"Oh," said Ben. "Well, nice shot."

Lee Trevino is exactly the opposite of Ben. If he tried to go into a trance like Ben, he might explode. He likes to talk during a round. He'll talk to anyone who will listen. Hell, he'll talk to anyone whether they'll listen or not. It's his way of keeping the pressure off himself until it's time to pull a club and make the shot.

One year in the PGA Championship, Lee was paired with the late Davis Love, Jr., the father of Davis Love III, who is such a fine young player on the tour. Davis, Jr., was a good player, but he was very nervous and intense on the course.

As they waited to tee off on the first hole, Lee jabbered away and kept on talking as they headed down the first fairway. Finally, as politely as he could, Davis told Lee that if it was all the same to him, Davis didn't like to talk during the round.

"That's okay, Davis," said Lee. "I'll do enough talking for both of us."

And he did.

Everyone is different, but the approach to concentration that works best for the majority of golfers lies somewhere between Ben's and Lee's methods, and probably closer to Lee's since golf is supposed to be a time when you get together with your friends.

When I'm playing, I try to stay in a "cool-mad" state of mind. As a competitor, I'm out there to beat the other guy, but you can't maintain that attitude of intense concentration for an entire round. By the end of four hours or so, you'll have one of the worst headaches in history.

My suggestion is that you carve the round up into thirty-second pockets of concentration. You can talk to your friends, watch the birds and chipmunks, do anything you like until it's time to play— and then you can begin to concentrate. From the time you study the conditions and pull a club from your bag, until the ball has landed, that's your period of concentration.

Realistically, there are very few Ben Hogans around who can go off in their own world for hours at a stretch, but I'm pretty sure most people can handle it for thirty seconds at a time.

"Visualize" and Improve

There's an old saying, "Mind over matter," and lately, as psychologists become more involved in sports at every level, people are beginning to better understand the role that your mind and your imagination plays, not only in golf, but in day-to-day life itself.

Back when I started playing, the only doctor you ever went to was a guy who would help you get over a flu or a bad back. I don't suppose anyone ever thought much about going to a doctor to understand what was going on inside your brain. But even back then I knew that if I used my powers of imagination and visualization, it certainly would help improve my game.

I use visualization in two ways: First, during a round I visualize both my swing and the shot I'm trying to hit. Second, off the course I visualize the round I'm about to play. Let me talk about the second part first.

Whenever I had an important round to play the following day, I would set aside some quiet time the night before to think about what lay ahead. I'd find a comfortable chair in a quiet room and just sit there with my eyes closed, imagining the round I faced. I'd begin on the first tee, visualizing the hole and actually seeing myself play my tee shot, second shot and so on. Naturally, I'd see only good things happening because you must do everything you can to put yourself in a positive frame of mind.

When I'm on the golf course, visualization takes on a more complicated, and more important, form.

As I'm preparing to select a club, I see in my mind's eye exactly the type of shot I need to play. Maybe it's a high, soft fade. Maybe I need to knock the ball down out of the wind and let it run up to the hole. Once I've determined the shot I want to play, I pull the club from my bag. Obviously, again I'm seeing only a successful shot here. I take note of where the trouble is, but I don't dwell on it and I never—never—make trouble the last thing I look at before I swing.

Once I've determined the shot and pulled the club, I visualize the swing I need to make to pull it off. In this way, my muscles and brain are working on the same wavelength. Once I've got a mental image for the shot I need to hit, I go ahead and make a practice swing to let my muscles feel what the swing feels like, and to establish whatever little swing key I use for this type of shot.

At this point, I'd like to interject a bit of advice for accomplished players who are able to pull off a variety of shots.

I believe it's a good idea to always try to work the ball one way or the other in a shot—first, because a straight ball is the toughest

"See your shot into the hole" by visualizing it before you make it.

1

2

3

4

5

6

7

to hit; second, because trying to hit a fade or draw forces you to focus just a little bit more intently than usual, and this helps your concentration. Finally, by turning the ball one way or the other, you give yourself a little bigger target because you are, hopefully, turning the ball away from the most serious trouble on the hole.

Either way, my last piece of advice concerning visualization is to always use it to build up your confidence. If you've hit a poor shot, don't leave on a sour note. Gary Player is the best example of this.

Nobody ever believed more in the power of positive thinking, or got more out of his golf game, than Gary Player from South Africa. The next time you get a chance to watch him play, pay careful attention when he misses a shot. Rather than storm off down the fairway with steam pouring from his ears, he'll stand back, visualize a good swing and a good shot, and even make a good practice swing so that next time he faces a similar shot, the image and feeling his body will have will be a positive one rather than one of failure.

Some Trouble Shots

If there is one thing that is certain in golf, it's that it is seldom going to be a day at the beach. Everyone gets his share of bad breaks along the way, and everyone gets himself into his share of trouble.

The key is knowing how to cope with trouble without letting it get the best of you. The first rule is to stay calm. Panicking isn't going to help matters a bit. Study your options and weight the risks versus the rewards of whatever shot you face.

True, there will be times where you just won't have a shot you can play safely. When that's the case, all you can do is take your medicine and move on, consoling yourself that eventually the breaks even out. Most of the time, however, with knowledge and practice, you can cope with most of the trouble shots you'll face. In this section I'll give you the knowledge I've learned over the years. What you do with it, and how much you practice it, is up to you.

Playing from a Divot   There are probably worse feelings on the golf course than nailing a drive down the heart of the fairway, only to reach the ball and find it sitting down in a divot. For years, Lee Trevino and other players have argued that the rules should be changed so you can move a ball out of a divot. After all, the game's tough enough without punishing someone for something that wasn't his fault. I think Lee has a good point, but I wouldn't bet the farm on the rule being changed.

Either way, while it is a tough break, you can play the shot without doing too much damage to your score. The key is making a solid, sharp descending blow on the ball, gouging it out of the divot and sending it scampering on its way.

You have to realize that it's not a shot to play with either a fairway wood or a long iron because you need to make such a strong, downward blow. Those clubs don't have enough loft to let you pull the shot off.

Address the ball the same way you would to hit a low, punch shot (page 67). The ball is back in your stance and your hands are ahead of the ball. Take the club back straight away from the ball and hit down sharply on the ball, with your hands leading the clubhead into the hitting area. It is crucial that you strike the ball first.

Like a punch shot, you have to give this shot plenty of air, since it's going to come out hot and running. But it will come out and allow you a play, and that's what a trouble shot is all about.

Playing from a Fairway Bunker   Occasionally you'll be watching a tournament on television and you'll hear a player hit a drive and then say, "Get in the bunker." If you're like most weekend players, you can't imagine a worse place to be, and with good reason. Nobody ever explained the fundamentals of playing this shot for you. For the pros, being in a bunker is often preferable to being in the deep rough they face in the major championships.

There are two things to look for right off the bat when you've hit a ball into a fairway bunker. The first is the lie. Again, the lie always dictates what kind of shot you'll be able to play. If you have a poor lie, you have to swallow hard and pitch the ball back into the fairway.

Secondly, you have to check to see how high the lip of the bunker is, and how far back from the lip your ball is sitting.

The absolute first rule when you are in a bunker is to get the ball out. This is not the time to get greedy or try to be a hero, only to hit a poor shot and plug the ball up in the lip.

However, if you do have a good lie and clearing the lip isn't a problem, the mechanics of the shot are fairly routine.

This is another case where you want to do everything possible to ensure that you strike the ball first. If you hit this shot fat, there's a good chance you'll leave the ball in the bunker and give yourself another chance at the shot.

When I walk in the bunker and address the ball, I work my feet into the sand. This gives me a solid base to play from, and also gives me a feel for how firm the sand is. The rules don't allow you to build a lie or test the sand, but they do let you work your feet into the sand, and if, in doing that, you sense that the sand is firm or soft, well, I say that's not testing, that's just paying attention to the world around you.

Since you have lowered your feet in the sand, you must remember to choke down slightly on the club to help prevent yourself from hitting the shot fat. Play the ball back in your stance to help ensure that you strike the ball first, and limit your weight shift to avoid losing your balance.

Once you become comfortable with this shot, you can experiment with hitting a cut shot, which will get the ball higher into the air and help it land more softly. Play the ball slightly more forward in your stance, and open both your stance and the clubface. Swing the club back away from the ball slightly to the outside of the target line and cock your wrists early in the backswing. This will help you make a more steeply descending swing. But keep in mind, the key is striking the ball first—and making sure that no matter what else you do, you get the ball out of the sand.

Buried Lie in a Bunker   When you play on a course with very fine, soft sand, you run the risk of the ball burying in the bunker. This

*Hitting out of a trap doesn't have to be disastrous,
especially if you're hitting up an uphill lie.*

1

2

3

4

5

6

7

8

is the so-called fried egg lie, and while it is a difficult shot, it does give you a few options in playing it.

It's unusual to get this lie in a fairway bunker, but if you do, it is one case where your hands are tied. All you can do is pitch back into the fairway and try to limit the damage. The lie won't let you do anything else.

If you're in a greenside bunker, you must realize that no matter what you do, or how well you play the shot, this ball is not going to check, so allow for plenty of roll and don't be surprised or angry when you get it.

You address the ball as you would for any greenside bunker shot. Open your stance and open the clubface. The ball is going to come out in the direction the blade is aimed, not your stance, so aim accordingly. And open your blade before you grip the club. Too often, people grip the club and then turn their hands to open the blade. Inevitably, this causes the clubface to close down at impact.

Since you want to hit this shot on an outside-to-in swing path, you should take the club back away from the ball outside the target line with an earlier-than-usual wrist cock. The deeper the ball is buried, the more sharply descending your swing must be. Remember, the ball tends to come out of the sand on a trajectory similar to the path the clubhead entered the sand, so with this shot you want to make as steep a downswing as possible, accelerating the clubhead under the ball. As I said, the shot will have a lot of roll to it, so the smart play is often to play away from the hole. After all, it doesn't do you a lot of good to get the ball out of one bunker, only to have it roll through the green into a bunker lurking on the other side.

There is another option you have when you face a buried lie. Since a pitching wedge has a sharp leading edge and virtually no bounce, it will cut deeply through the sand and dig the ball out. This is a particularly good shot if the sand is firm or wet.

Set up to the ball with both your stance and the blade square, and with your hands slightly ahead of the ball. All these precautions will help prevent the clubhead from bouncing behind the ball and skulling the shot, and will help the clubhead dig under the ball and get it out of the bunker. This is a shot that takes a lot of practice, both so you can pull it off successfully and so you'll know how the ball will react. It's a specialty shot, but one that's useful to have.

Uneven Lies in a Bunker If every bunker shot was played from a nice, level lie, they wouldn't be so bad. The problem is that every round or so you find yourself facing either an uphill or downhill lie, and those are rarely shots that you've practiced or feel comfortable with.

Actually, an uphill lie is a pretty simple shot once you get the hang of it. You must ensure that your feet are completely worked into the sand, since this will help you guard against swaying on the shot. The secret is aligning your shoulders to the shape of the slope. Your right shoulder must be considerably lower than your left. Your stance and the clubface are square.

You take the club back directly from the ball to about shoulder height and then drive down sharply into the ball. The ball will jump straight up and land softly, although without much spin, and you don't have to concern yourself with the follow-through. There probably won't be one. Playing from a downhill lie, however, is a horse of a different color. There are hard shots and then there are really hard shots—and this can be hard enough to ruin your whole day.

Again, it's crucial that you dig in and get yourself as strong a stance as possible. This shot is so awkward that you must constantly guard against losing your balance. Obviously, the majority of your weight is going to be set on your forward foot, to help keep you from falling over during the swing. Don't even dream of shifting any weight. Just plant your feet, flex your knees and, as much as possible, align your shoulders with the slope of the bunker. Your shoulders are important to this shot because the more you can align them to the slope, the more you'll be able to swing the clubhead along that slope. With this shot, you want to open the blade and try to slide it along the slope and under the ball, accelerating well through the ball. You must guard against the ball going to the right on this shot, and you must be very careful that you don't blade the ball, which is easy to do from this awkward lie.

This is not a shot to get fancy with. It's one of the toughest shots in the game, and anytime you can get the ball out and on the putting surface, you've done a good job.

Ball Above Your Feet   The first thing you must recognize in facing this shot is that the ball is going to go to the left of where you are aiming it and it is going to run like a son of a gun. Depending on how far above your feet the ball is, the swing can be almost more like a baseball swing than a golf swing.

Take a nice, wide stance and choke down on the club as much as possible to give yourself all the control you can get. You want to play this with the stiffest wrists possible, and concentrate on keeping the clubhead moving toward the target as long as you can, resisting the temptation to swing around your body and pull the shot well to the left.

Ball Below Your Feet   There are tougher shots in golf, but none as awkward. No matter what you do, this shot is not going to be pretty.

My best advice is to flex your knees as much as possible, trying to make up the distance between you and the ball. Whatever distance you can't make up in this manner, you'll have to make do with bending from the waist. It will also help if you widen your stance as much as you can, since this will not only lower you, but also will give you the strongest possible base to play from.

You can't do anything fancy with your swing. Just try to make the best contact you can. You must make sure, however, that you don't allow the clubhead to touch the sand either at address or on the backswing, since this is a penalty—and easy to do under such awkward circumstances.

Finally, here's a bit of advice that may help you with this shot. Whenever I have Wilson make up a sand wedge for me, I have them put in a shaft that is an inch or so longer than the standard sand wedge shaft. This gives me a little help when I'm facing one of these awkward shots, and I can always choke down slightly for more normal lies.

The Long Bunker Shot   There's hardly a golf telecast that goes by during which an announcer doesn't say that the long bunker shot is "the toughest shot in the game." There's a good reason for that: It just might be.

In order to hit this shot, you need to make a long, full swing and that opens the door to either skulling the shot or hitting it fat.

I play the shot by positioning the ball slightly forward in my stance and closing the blade slightly. A good rule of thumb for bunker play is that the more you open the blade, the higher—and shorter—the ball will carry. On this shot, you need to control the distance the ball flies by manipulating the blade at address. Since you are going for distance and not height, you also want to make more of a U-shaped swing, as opposed to the V-shaped swing you'd make to hit the ball high.

The shot I've just described takes a lot of skill and practice to perfect, but I have another suggestion that may help: Just change clubs.

As long as you have a clean lie, I'd suggest trying a pitching wedge, 9-iron, 8-iron or even 7-iron, and simply pitching the ball to the green, just as you would from the fairway. The distance you have to carry the ball and the height of the lip will determine which club you use.

The mechanics are fairly simple. Dig your feet in slightly for stability and play the ball back in your stance with your hands ahead of the ball. Take a short backswing and hit down on the ball cleanly, making sure that the clubhead strikes the ball before the sand. Don't break your wrists. Just make sure that your hands have led the clubhead into the hitting area.

With practice, this is a shot that you can become very comfortable with very quickly. Because it is a shorter swing, it's a safer shot than trying to explode the ball with a sand club. You may be giving up a little spin, but when you think about how safe and easy this shot is, it's not a bad trade-off.

Playing from the Rough   When you miss a green and the ball nestles down into the rough, the first problem you face is not being sure how the ball is going to come out. That confusion leads to indecision: How hard should I swing? How far will the ball carry and how far will it run?

Earlier in this section I explained the mechanics for playing an explosion shot from a bunker, and that's the shot you want to hit here.

Address the ball with an open clubface and stance, with the ball positioned off your left heel. This shot needs to be played with a strong, descending blow, so you need to make the V-shaped swing we discussed earlier, with the club being taken away from the ball outside the target line and your wrists cocking quickly. A good mental image is that you are going to drop the clubhead right down behind the ball.

Since the grass will come between the clubhead and the ball, this shot will have overspin and will hit the green running. There's not much you can do except allow for it—and practice this shot as much as possible. With practice, you'll be better able to gauge how the ball will react from certain lies, and that knowledge will give you some idea just how much you can get away with in competition.

Playing from Hard Pan   Of all the so-called trouble shots in this section, this is the least troublesome. When you find yourself playing from a bare lie, the one thing you want to guard against is the clubhead bouncing off the ground behind the ball, skulling the shot. To prevent this, the first thing you should do is leave your sand wedge in the bag, since its wide flange and built-in bounce are designed to make the club do just that—bounce through the sand. Instead, go with a pitching wedge or 9-iron, depending on how much ground you have to carry.

The mechanics of the shot are pretty straightforward. Play the

When caught in the rough, force yourself to drop that clubhead right behind the ball.

1

2

3

4

5

6

7

8

ball back in your stance, with your hands ahead of the ball, both at address and at impact. Play this shot with a square blade and a slightly open stance. By squaring the blade, you reduce the bounce on the club, and by playing from an open stance, you get your hips out of the way before the swing even begins.

The shot requires a short backswing and plenty of acceleration through the ball. Just punch down crisply on the ball, and don't allow your wrists to break or roll over. It's like a long pitch shot—and it's nothing to fear.

A Few Short Game Thoughts

In the last section we covered most of the basics for any shot you'll face around the greens. Armed with those basics, a little imagination and a lot of practice, you'll be able to save a bundle of strokes when you do miss greens.

In this section I'd like to share just some general theories I've developed about the short game.

The first theory has to do with club selection for chip and pitch shots around the green. Three factors determine how these shots are played: speed, height and spin.

Speed refers to how hard the ball is hit to carry the distance to the hole. With practice, I believe anyone can comfortably become a pretty good judge of how hard he must hit a shot to have it pay off.

Height refers to how high you need to hit the ball to have it carry a certain length and either land softly or release and run to the hole. Learning to control the height of your shots is a little more complicated than learning to determine how hard you should hit it. To control the height of a shot, you have to consider the club you want to hit, how much you want to open or close the blade, and the shape and path of the swing you're going to make.

Spin is the result of the combination of the first two factors. How hard you hit the ball, coupled with what you do to achieve height, will determine the amount of spin you put on the ball. For that reason, spinning the ball is the most complicated part of the short game, and the most difficult to control.

This explanation lies at the root of two of my strongest beliefs about the short game, and if you'll hear me out, I think I can make a pretty convincing case that some of the things you're doing now may be costing you strokes along the way.

Take a minute to think about both your chipping and pitching game and your friends' games. If you're like most amateurs I've seen over the years, you have a favorite club to chip and sometimes pitch with, and that's the club you stick with, come hell or high water. If that's the case, I think both you and your friends are wrong—and apparently, so do most of the guys on tour.

All it takes is a little common sense to figure out that it's a lot easier and predictable to change clubs in order to control speed, height and spin than it is to stick with one club and try to vary your swing. I don't care how good you are, or how lucky you think that favorite club of yours is, I say you're making life hard for yourself.

Let me review the basics of chipping and pitching, and then I've got a challenge for you to try.

The most important factor in becoming a good chipper and pitcher of the ball is making crisp, solid contact time after time. If you're hitting the ball with a closed clubface one time and an open blade the next, there's no way you can accurately judge how the ball is going to come off the clubface.

Here's my foolproof method for solid contact, and you can practice this at home, in the office, in the backyard or at the golf course. First, you want to address the ball with a slightly open stance. By pulling your left foot away from the target line, you're already taking your hips out of the way. Play the ball back in your stance and position your hands ahead of the ball. Keep them this way throughout the shot. Do not ever let the clubhead pass your hands—period. Bend your knees comfortably and position your feet closely together, with slightly more weight over your left foot. This will help you make the descending blow the shot demands. The clubface should be square. If you open the clubface, you are going to add a left-to-right spin to the ball, and for right now we are trying to reduce, not add, spin to your shots.

Take the clubhead squarely away from the ball, neither inside nor outside the line. If it helps, lay a ruler down behind the ball and practice taking the club back along the ruler until you get the feel for a proper takeaway. The most important part of this shot is at impact. You must make a crisply descending blow, with your hands leading the clubhead into the ball. Avoid any wristiness, since that breeds inconsistency. Since your sole focus at this stage of the game is in making solid contact, I don't think you should concern yourself with a follow-through. Instead, just concentrate on trapping down on the ball at the same point in your swing, time after time.

Once you have practiced enough to feel comfortable with this technique, go to a practice green with several clubs, from a 6-iron to a pitching wedge. Begin by hitting balls with the pitching wedge and move steadily down until you are making the same solid, crisp contact with the 6-iron as you have with the rest of the clubs. Don't worry about chipping to a specific target. Instead, observe how easy it is to vary the height and distance of the shot simply by hitting different clubs with the same swing.

Once you have gotten this far, pick a variety of targets to chip to, some close by, some farther away. Again, keep in mind that what you are striving to do is control the distance through club selection and speed, eliminating spin as much as possible. A good way to do this is to keep in mind this saying: Maximum ground time, minimum air time. You want that ball on the green, rolling smoothly, as soon as possible. You don't want to have to worry about how much or how little a shot is going to check up because of the spin you've put on it.

Many people are confused by the difference between a chip shot and a pitch. Here's the best and simplest way I can describe it: A chip is a shot that runs along the green farther than it flies through the air. A pitch is just the opposite.

The swing for a pitch shot is very similar to a chip, except that it is a longer, softer swing. Still, solid, consistent contact is what you're after, and that requires a descending blow. Don't fall in the trap that many amateurs do, which is trying to help the ball into the air with a wristy, scooping motion. They have no chance and neither will you.

To play a pitch shot, you again open your stance and vary the height of the shot by the degree that you open the clubface. Unlike a chip shot, your hands are not quite as far ahead of the ball, largely because the ball is not positioned as far back in your stance. For a pitch, play the ball forward, near your left instep.

The key to pulling this shot off is making a full, long swing and accelerating through the hitting area. Unlike a chip shot, you want to make a nice, high finish. The higher your finish, the better your chances of hitting a nice, soft pitch.

Along with varying your clubs to control the distance you hit your shots around the green, my other firm belief is that people should forget about using a sand wedge as a pitching club.

I know that the boys on tour do the bulk of their pitch shots with sand wedges, but there are two reasons for that. First, they are very skilled and have a lot of time to practice. More importantly, though, they use sand wedges that are actually designed to do double duty as pitching clubs. They have the manufacturers grind down the width of the sole and severely grind away much of the bounce. They can get away with using a club like this because they are so skilled out of the bunkers. The average Joe would spend the day in the bunker if he had to try to play with a club as unforgiving as this.

On the other hand, if the pros tried to play sand shots with a wedge suited for the weekend player, they'd have a tough time getting used to the excessive bounce.

What's the solution? For some of the pros it's using the sand clubs they have today, but I think many of them—and all amateurs—would be better served using a pitching wedge.

For one thing, it's a more forgiving club because the design won't let it skid into the ball on a fat hit as easily as a sand wedge will. You can also hit more shots with a pitching wedge. If you need to hit the ball low and running, you can set your hands ahead of the ball and trap it, making the club play like an 8-iron. If you need to hit it high, you can open the blade and slide it under the club, tossing the ball softly into the air.

Now this kind of shotmaking takes a lot of time and practice, and awfully good nerves. For those reasons, I like to see most people stick with the basics. But if I had a choice in seeing my pro-am partners forsake a good sand club in order for them to play pitch shots with a sand wedge, I'd rather see them become comfortable experimenting with a pitching wedge. After all, it is called a pitching wedge, isn't it?

Now for my challenge: I truly believe that if you make the two changes we've discussed here—varying your clubs and not your swing, and forsaking your sand wedge as a pitching club—you'll be a much more consistent player around the greens. But it won't be easy to give up your favorite club. I'd like to challenge you to try it my way for at least a month. I mean really give this a chance by practicing and putting it to the test on the course. It will take time, and you'll make your share of mistakes, but in the long run you'll be better off. I guarantee it. It worked for me.

The Players I've Known
The Big-Money Era

*P*eople often ask me if I think players today are overpaid. Not at all. All I wish is that I was twenty years old and had about five years to make my mark. Give me five good years and I could look forward to a lifetime of hunting and fishing.

I've played with many of these players, since I was still out on the tour when they came up as rookies in the early '70s. I remember guys like Lanny Wadkins, Tom Kite and Ben Crenshaw when they were fresh-faced little kids right out of college. I'm familiar with some of the younger players from seeing them at tournaments like the Masters or from watching them on television.

I don't think players in this era are any better than the best players over the years, but I do think there are more good players. And I think the fact that they are playing for so much money gives them a tremendous edge, since they have less pressure on them week after week. That's one reason the scores are so low. Of course, the fact that equipment is so much better and the courses are so well maintained also has a lot to do with it.

Thinking about these players, how they play and handle themselves both on and off the course, gives me a lot of confidence in the future of the tour and the future of the game. With folks like this around, golf will keep growing like gangbusters.

Paul Azinger   Now here's an example of a player with a self-made swing who has played enough so that his swing will work for him. He's got some flaws that you wouldn't teach anyone, but the overall package seems to work for him, and he's smart enough not to let anyone change his game.

In some respects, Paul reminds me of Ben Hogan because he worked so hard to find a good swing. He's also got a lot of heart, and that's what you need to become a champion. The kid has a lot of fire, and that will take you a long way.

I remember watching him in the 1987 British Open at Muirfield. He lost his composure coming down the final stretch on Sunday, and Nick Faldo came away with the trophy. That's the kind of thing that happens the first few times you get in contention in a big tournament. What I like about Paul is that he didn't let that break his spirit. He'll be able to handle the pressure a whole lot better next time around.

Seve Ballesteros   Seve might be the best in the world right now. You'd be hard-pressed to find anyone who could beat him very often.

Seve plays with a lot of passion. He wants to eat you alive on the course, and he's probably more dangerous when he's down, since he's got so much pride that he refuses to give in.

He was clearly the top player in the world a few years ago, but I think he dropped off a little bit, which is only natural. Once you've fought your way to the top, there's only one place to go. Still, the mark of a great player is in his ability to come back, and Seve has done that more than once.

Seve has a lot of talent. He's a good driver and a wonderful putter. His fundamentals are very sound. If there's one weakness in his swing, it's that he bends a little too much from the waist. That makes it difficult to keep the club on the proper line throughout the swing. He can get away with that more than most because he's a better athlete than the majority of players.

I think Seve will go on to become one of the all-time greats. He's got the game and the desire. I think he's at the point where he's playing for the history books and not the bankbooks. That combination will make him a hard player to beat.

Chip Beck   Here's a good example of how winning breeds winning. Chip has been a good player for a long time, but he had a bad case of "second-place-itis." He'd get close to winning, but he just couldn't quite pull it off. Once he did win, though, he got the confidence to keep on winning.

I think he's got a nice, compact swing. It works well for him because he's as strong as a bull. A swing like his will cut down on ball-striking mistakes, but you have to guard against it getting too short as you get older. I've always thought that the players whose swings aged the best were players who had long swings to begin with. Look at guys like Don January or Gene Littler.

Chip is a very good putter, and that's another area where he's gotten a big boost from his confidence. When you're winning, you expect to make every putt you look at. When you're finishing second, that little man inside your head keeps finding ways to miss, especially down the stretch. I think Chip has taken that little man and sent him on a long vacation.

Mark Calcavecchia   When this kid first broke through, people said it was because of square grooves. That's crazy. He's a big, strong player with a damned good swing. If you watch him from down the line, you see that the club comes down on the same path it goes up. That's one sure sign of a good swing. He doesn't reroute it along the way. Of course, he swings so hard that he kind of flounders a bit at the end, but that's okay.

He's an aggressive player, but that's how you have to be to win out on tour these days. If you get to three under and try to protect your lead, the boys will go past you as if you're standing still. Being aggressive will cost you some tournaments, but it'll win you a bunch more in the long run.

People forget one thing about this boy: He may be a thrasher, but he's got a nice touch around the greens. He's a good putter and chipper. The two usually go hand in hand, but when you combine a good touch with a long hitter who is aggressive, you've got the making of a player who'll be around for a while—and I think Mark will be.

Fred Couples   Here's a mystery man if there ever was one. He plays as if he doesn't have a nerve in his body or a care in the world.

Fred has a very unusual swing. He sort of folds his arms through the swing, but he's so damn loose that he gets tremendous acceleration through the hitting area. He's very long, and that gives him an edge.

I don't think Fred is what you'd call an outstanding putter, but he makes his share and he does seem to make them under pressure.

I know there are people who believe that if Fred would just bear down and get a little tougher, he'd win a lot more. I don't know. I think you've got to play your own game. If you're out there trying to be someone else, then you're acting, not golfing, and you're not going to be around for long.

Ben Crenshaw   Ben is another one of those players whom people think may just be too nice for his own good. He's just so eager to please people and not hurt anyone's feelings that they say it takes away from his golf game. Well hell, that's the way he was raised. You can't expect someone to go against his grain and still be successful. I don't know what people think about sometimes.

I do think that occasionally Ben gets too hard on himself. All good players are perfectionists, but you've got to accept the bad breaks and missed shots. For someone nicknamed Gentle Ben, he can get pretty hot with himself, but that's part of the spark you need if you're going to win.

Everyone knows that Ben is one of the best putters we have on tour, and has been throughout his career. It's not surprising that he has such a good short game because he plays so much by feel and instinct. If you tried to change him in any way, you'd run the risk of wrecking his game.

Like all top players, Ben has suffered through his share of slumps. In his case, they were tougher to shake because everyone was so eager to help that they overloaded him with advice. Finally, he just went back to doing what came naturally, and he got his confidence back.

Ben has been a little wild off the tee throughout his career, but as he's gotten older his swing has naturally shortened up a little. That's helped his ball striking and made him a much more consistent player. It may be that we haven't seen the best of Ben quite yet.

Nick Faldo   I don't know all that much about Nick because he hasn't really played enough on our tour. I understand that he plans to begin playing a full schedule over here, and I think that will help him get the most out of his game. You've got to play with the best players before you can beat them. Europe has some outstanding golfers, but they don't have the depth our tour does and I doubt if they ever will.

One thing that does impress me about Nick is his temperament. He seems to keep his composure very well. When he faced Curtis Strange in the playoff for the 1988 U.S. Open, he played well enough from tee to green, but just had one of those days when the putts wouldn't drop. He seemed to take it very well and not let it rattle him. After winning the Masters, I believe the next couple years could tell how good he can ultimately become.

Tom Kite When Tom first came out on tour, we'd occasionally play practice rounds together, and I noticed that he was always paying close attention, trying to learn as much as he could.

I think Tom is very smart and he's as hard a worker as there is on tour. In my opinion, that combination has paid off for him because he's about as consistent a player as you'll ever want to see. Year in and year out he's always near the top in money winnings, and he's a safe bet for at least one win a year.

My hunch is that Tom will win for a long time. He's in good shape, is stronger than you might suspect, and he keeps fine-tuning his game, adding bits of polish here and there. And there are few players who think their way around a course better than he does. I believe people could learn a lot from watching him on the course.

Bernhard Langer You could count the number of outstanding players Germany has produced on one hand and still have plenty of fingers left. That Bernhard Langer is as good as he is tells you something about his desire and mental toughness.

People sometimes criticize his swing and some of his fundamentals. His grip is unorthodox, and I'm not sure I'd teach anyone to collapse the way he does following impact. But if you watch him, the one thing I like a lot is how steady he keeps his head. It remains motionless, which makes it a whole lot easier to make solid contact.

I'd like to say he'll win his battle with the yips, but I'm afraid that once you've had them, you've got them. I think Bernhard will have stretches when he'll be capable of outstanding golf, but I think he'll also have more than his share of troubles on the greens, which is a damn shame for someone so young and so talented.

Davis Love III It's a funny thing about young Davis. His late father, Davis, Jr., was a friend of mine, a good player and a fine teacher. He asked me to play nine holes with Davis when he was in high school. I wasn't exactly overwhelmed. He was good, but I didn't think he was going to be a world-beater.

The next thing I knew, J.C. was telling me about this kid on tour who hit the ball farther than anyone he'd ever seen and was supposed to be the next superstar. That turned out to be Davis, and having seen him play, I think J.C. may have been onto something.

Davis is very long, and length gives a player a big edge over the field, particularly as courses get longer on tour. What people forget is that a long hitter not only has an edge off the tee, but he's longer with each club. Even if you're nothing better than an average putter, if you keep hitting two clubs less into greens than the rest of the field, you're bound to make more than your share of birdies.

People often try to make comparisons between players from one generation, and the other day a fellow asked me just how long a hitter young Davis really is. All I know is that the 8th hole at Oakmost is a 245-yard par 3. In my prime, I hit that green with a 1-iron, which was unheard-of at the time. Davis hit a 1-iron on the same hole. He carried it into the trees behind the green. That's long enough for me.

Sandy Lyle   You'd never say Sandy has a classic swing, but his swing does suit him because he's a big, strong player who can get away with hooding the clubface. He blocks a lot of shots and occasionally hits a lot of pulls. Fortunately for him, his short game is so good that he can make up for any missed shots he might hit in the course of a round.

Sandy has a very placid attitude about him. You'd never confuse him with Seve. But placid shouldn't be confused with weak because he has a streak of iron in him. He showed that in the 1988 Masters, when he came back from near-disaster on the 12th on Sunday, and then birdied 18 from the fairway bunker on the final hole. Unless you've been there, you can't fully appreciate how good his second shot really was.

Sandy now has a British Open and a Masters win under his belt. I wouldn't bet that those will be the last majors he wins either.

Johnny Miller   For a while in the 1970s, Johnny might have been our best player. He was long, he was a wonderful iron player, and he could putt.

When people ask what happened to him, I think it's a two-part answer. First, he moved to Utah, and at one point took some time off to chop wood and clear some land. He got very strong, but in golf you need flexible strength, not brute strength. It changed his body and affected the way he swung the club. As a result, he didn't strike the ball as well, and that put a lot of pressure on his putting. That's the second part of the answer. His putting finally failed him, and the combination of the two did him in.

I'm not sure that Johnny didn't just get bored with the game. He played so well for so long that I think he lost interest. He had a way of doing that if things weren't going well.

I recall being paired with him in 1974 at Los Angeles. He wasn't in contention, and frankly, he was just kind of dogging it. Finally, I took him aside as we walked up a fairway near the close of the round.

"Look, Johnny," I said. "I wouldn't say any of this if I didn't care about you, but these people have paid good money to see you play your best. This round may not mean much to you, but I think you owe it to these people and yourself to give it your all."

I wasn't sure how he'd take it, but later that night he called and thanked me for the advice. That showed me that Johnny was as classy a guy as I had thought he was—and he certainly had a great run there for a while.

Greg Norman   People can debate who the best current player is, but I'm pretty sure the best player with the worst luck has to be Greg Norman. What are the odds of a player losing both the Masters and the PGA in playoffs when his opponents holed shots on him on the last hole? Yet it happened to Greg.

We all know that luck can run hot and cold in golf, but I'd say he's about due for some good luck. He's a big, strong player, and Jack Nicklaus thinks he's the best in the world today, so that should count for something.

I think Greg would do himself a favor if he stayed and played in the States a bit more. Travel has improved, but it still takes a lot out of you and your game.

People often criticize his career, pointing out that he's won just one of the four majors, the British Open. But they forget that he's lost in playoffs in the three others. One shot here and there and it's a different story. To me, the real test is how he copes with the disappointment of losing in those playoffs. The great champions have all come back from defeats, and I think Greg Norman will, too.

Joey Sindelar   I like this young man a lot. He's a strong player, with plenty of length and a good touch around the green. He comes across as very down to earth. He also seems to really enjoy the game, which isn't always the case. A lot of players look at it as just a way to make a living. Joey really appears to like it out on tour. He must, since he plays more tournaments than almost anyone else.

If there's one thing I'd guard against, it would be playing too much. It's tough to take a week off when there's so much money at stake, both in purses and in bonuses, but it's very easy to get stale out on tour. When that happens you fall into some bad habits and those lead to slumps. I don't know anyone, in any walk of life, who can work every week without the job taking its toll. And golfers are no different from anyone else.

J. C. Snead   In a way, I think J.C. might have been better off if his name had been Smith. That way people wouldn't spend as much time comparing the two of us.

People assume that I spent a lot of time with J.C. when he was coming up, but actually I never did play with him until he'd already turned pro. He was a hell of an athlete as a kid, and even played professional baseball for a while.

I think J.C. has as much talent as anyone on the tour. I've tried to get him to play on more of an even keel, not getting too high or too low. I think that would help him a lot. It's like a boxer. The first thing he tries to do is get his opponent mad so that he'll punch himself out early.

One thing about J.C. that most people don't recognize is that he's a wonderful student of the golf swing. A lot of the guys on tour come to him for help. I don't reckon that he plans to quit playing the tour for quite a while, but if he wanted to try his hand at teaching, I think he'd be damn good.

Payne Stewart   I think the only thing holding Payne back is his putting. He misses more of the 5- and 10-footers you need to make to win than any other top player I've seen. He's got a good swing and temperament for the game, but when he gets to the greens, it's as if he were in another world. He aims one way and putts another. On top of that, he gets the putter up on the toe, which means the sweet spot isn't even the size of a dime.

As good a player as Payne is, I think if he'd get himself squared away with a decent putting technique, and then give himself enough time to develop a little confidence, he'd be a tough player to beat.

Curtis Strange   I've known Curtis since he was about twelve years old. His dad, Tom, worked in the shop for me at the Greenbrier. His dad was a pretty good player in his own right.

Curtis has always been very hard on himself, but that's what it took for him to get to this point in his career. That's just how tough the game is at this level, and how much it demands from you.

Apart from all his skill and desire, Curtis has a good build for the game. He can get plenty of length while still making a controlled swing that will hold up for a long time. It's like a car with a big engine: You don't need to rev it up as high to get to a comfortable cruising speed.

I get a kick out of people who say that we Americans can't dominate the game anymore. It seems to me that Curtis and a couple of the other guys can give anyone you want all he can handle.

Hal Sutton   I think Hal plays well enough from tee to green, but I've never thought he was a good enough putter to ever dominate the game the way that some folks predicted he would. Like it or not, if you can't putt out here, you can't win—at least you can't win as often as you should with a good swing.

I don't believe in dwelling on a person's private life, but in Hal's case it's no secret that he's had a pretty rocky go of it with marriage. I bring this up only because the most successful players—the Jack Nicklauses and Arnold Palmers and the like—all have wives who are supportive and understanding. I hope that when Hal does get things squared away, his golf game will follow suit.

Bob Tway   I like his swing very much, and he does have a good build for the game. By winning the PGA, he proved that he can handle pressure, but for the past couple of years he seems to be forcing things. He doesn't appear comfortable and his concentration seems to be lacking.

I think that's all a part of finding yourself, and with all he has going for him, I think he's another player with a bright future.

Scott Verplank   To be honest with you, I was more impressed with his win in the 1988 Buick Open than I was when he won the 1985 Western Open as an amateur.

To win as an amateur, he didn't really have any pressure on him. Nobody expected him to win, so he could freewheel it. To hit the tour as a big name, and struggle, and then come back to win is impressive.

I think Scott will go on to have a good career. He's gotten over a big hump and he's a solid player. The next couple years should tell just how bright his future will truly be.

Lanny Wadkins   Nobody has more guts than Lanny. He hasn't got a textbook swing, but he makes it work for him, and more important, he has such tremendous belief in himself that he's been able to overcome a lot.

If you look back over his career, you see that when he hasn't been sick or injured, he's always in the running.

People say that Lanny never met a pin placement he wouldn't attack, and that's probably true. That's just his nature. Every now and then it catches up with him, just like a football team that passes, passes and passes again. But he's probably won more tournaments than he's lost by being true to his aggressive instincts.

I'll say this about Lanny: He can play as my partner anytime, and if we're serious about getting that Ryder Cup back, we'd better find a way to get a few guys like Lanny on the squad.

Tom Watson   Of all the great players I've seen, I'd say Tom has the most mechanical-looking swing of the bunch. He was never the best ball striker, but he could putt the lights out. In one tournament he missed the first seven greens and was still two under par.

Of course, if you live by the putter, you eventually die by it. He put so much pressure on his blade, and was so aggressive on the greens, that it was just a question of time before it caught up with him—just as it finally catches up with everyone.

Tom is a great champion, though. He's got a heart as big as anyone who has ever lived. And like every great champion, he'll find a way to come back and win again, just as he had to learn to win in the first place. And when he comes back, it will be with a vengeance.

Tom Weiskopf   Another mystery man. He had as good a swing as you'd ever want to see, and he could really control the ball. I'm just not sure he ever really had a passion for the game. I think he was such a perfectionist that it finally just drove him off the tour.

I'll say this in his favor: Tom probably hit more good putts that didn't go in than anyone I know. It was spooky. I keep hearing that he's going to come back out on tour, but I have my doubts. I think he's happy building courses, and when you've found something that makes you happy, it's tough to give it up.

Fuzzy Zoeller   He reminds me a lot of Jimmy Demaret. His uncle told me that Fuzzy really could care less if the ball goes in the hole, and maybe that's true. I do know he's got awfully good nerves.

The thing about Fuzzy is that everyone is his friend. He doesn't have strangers in his life, and people really respond to that. It's not the kind of thing you can fake.

Fuzzy has a very bad back, much worse than people think. In the end, it may force him to cut way back on his playing. That's a shame, both for him and golf. Guys like Jimmy and Fuzzy don't come along very often.

Course Strategy: Thinking Your Way to Lower Scores

*L*et's face it, not everyone has the physical gifts to be a superstar, but I believe that everyone can learn to think their way around a golf course. And once you learn to do that, you have a tremendous edge over the rest of the field.

Golf is a game of mistakes. Nobody hits every shot perfectly. Nobody gets all the luck running his or her way. But the players who get the most from their games are the ones who make the smallest mistakes—and the smallest number of them. In this section I'd like to concentrate on how you can improve your course management and begin saving strokes in a hurry.

I've touched on some of these areas in earlier sections, but I think this area of the game can help so many people that I'll briefly touch upon them again here.

Rate the Dangers Every hole has its share of trouble and danger, but not all trouble and danger is equal. There are some hazards you can deal with, and others that will jump up and grab you by the throat. When I study a hole from the tee, I run through a checklist of the trouble out there and plan my shots accordingly.

The first thing I want to avoid at all cost is out-of-bounds, since that is a stroke and distance penalty. In effect, hitting it OB costs you two shots. Next, I look to see if there's water on the hole. Putting the ball in water is going to cost you a stroke unless you get lucky enough to be able to play from it, and that's mighty unlikely.

After determining where the OB and water hazards are, I check to see where the trees are and how thick they are. Drive a ball into a thick stand of trees and you may get lucky and have a hole to play through—or you could be in there for a while. That's especially true if they are spruce trees, whose thick branches reach down to the ground. Hit a ball in a spruce and you are going to take a stroke for an unplayable lie. I avoid spruce trees like a 15-handicapper with a 1-iron in his bag. Rocks also fall in that category. Put a ball on the rocks and you might get lucky and have a lie, but more often than not you're looking at a drop and a shot.

Finally, I look at the fairway bunkers and the rough to see which is worse. A fairway bunker without much of a lip will get the edge over thick rough, simply because I'll probably have a better lie in the bunker. Put a ball in the rough and you may have to pitch back to the fairway—a half-shot mistake if you're lucky, but more likely you're going to go for a shot. Whatever the hazards, my first goal is to get the ball in the fairway at all costs, even if that means laying up off the tee with a 1-iron or fairway wood and leaving myself a longer approach into the green. When I stand on that tee, I want to know just how far I have to carry the ball to clear a bunker, and I don't want to be fooled by ripping a drive over a fairway bunker only to find that there wasn't a dime's worth of fairway behind it, and all I got for my efforts was a bad lie. It's also a good idea, and an often overlooked one at that, to study the slope of the fairway. If it's a gentle slope from right to left, for example, and there's no trouble down the left side, you can try to draw the ball into the slope and hope it will kick the ball forward for added distance. On the other hand, if there's trouble down the left side and you can fade a shot into that same slope, you'll take a lot of the trouble out of play.

When I plan my approach to the green, I run down a similar checklist. The first thing I want to take out of play is water. Next, I study where the hole is cut. Unless I need to gamble, I'll play conservatively, figuring that if I miss the shot, I want to make sure that I miss it away from the pin so that I'll have some green to work with on my recovery shot. Next, I again study the bunkers and the rough. Unless the bunkers are extremely deep, or the rough very thin, I'm probably better off in the bunker, where I've got a fighting chance at a lie that I can spin the ball from. If the rough is thin, that's not as big a concern because I should get a decent lie to play from.

Next, I want to always play to my strengths, which we discussed in the shotmaking chapter. While I'm comfortable working the ball either way, if I need the ball to sit down in a hurry, I'm going to fade the ball into the green to take advantage of the extra spin I'll get on the shot.

It's very important to play the best percentage shot as often as possible. Certainly, there are times when you can afford to attack and be a little more aggressive. If you are trailing a match with holes running out, or are in the early stages of a tournament when you still have plenty of time left to recover, then you can freewheel it a bit. In most cases, though, I feel you need at least a 65 to 70 percent chance of success before you try a shot—and greater than that if you're running the risk of bringing water into play.

When I'm planning my approach shot, the pin placement is my main consideration. If it is in a generous part of the green, I'll probably take a run at it. If it's tucked in behind a bunker, in a small part of the green, the smart play is to start the ball at the middle of the green and try to either fade or draw the ball into the pin. If the greens are firm, I'll probably just play to the middle, take my chances with a birdie putt, but be satisfied to walk off with a par.

On par 5s, strategy becomes a little more complicated. First, if there is water in front of the green, I won't even think about trying to hit the green in two unless I can comfortably carry the water with an iron. Second, if I decide to lay up, I want to lay up far enough from the green that my third shot will be with a full club. Too often I see people blast a second shot, knowing that they can't reach the green but trying to get as close as possible. They leave themselves with a delicate little half-wedge that's hard to hit and is hell on your nerves. If you're going to lay up, make sure you really lay up. When you try to get too cute in this game, it rears up and eats your lunch.

One final consideration when laying up, planning your drive or your tee shot on a par 3 is to give yourself the best angle into the green. If the pin is cut to the left side, most of the time you'll want to approach from the right, and vice versa. It gives you more green to work with and will usually take much of the trouble out of play.

My final piece of advice on course strategy is that it doesn't end when the round is over. I've always reviewed my rounds, thinking back on where I made mistakes.

I'd like to suggest that you do this: Keep a notebook and record how many fairways and greens you hit; how many times you got up-and-down from the rough and the bunkers; how many times you three-putted; when you missed shots, how you missed them—left or right, long or short. By keeping track of this kind of information, you'll have an accurate picture of your game—and what parts of your game you should be working on to improve.

Some Memorable Tournaments
Learning from a Loss

I think you learn something from every round you play, but it seems as if the lessons are magnified in the tournaments that are most important. Maybe it's because the pressure intensifies both your good and bad shots; your correct decisions as well as your mistakes.

In this section I'll deal with four tournaments I wish I could have another shot at—the U.S. Opens in 1937, 1939, 1947 and 1953. In all, I finished second in four Opens, and was in the top 10 thirteen times. If I could have shot 69 or better in the final round, I figure I would have won seven Opens.

Did never winning the Open bother me? Of course it did, although I always figured that it was predestined. I just wasn't meant to win the Open. It was as though the man upstairs said, "Sam, we gave you a lot, but we're not going to let you have a full plate." So be it, but it has caused me some restless nights of tossing and turning.

What follows are the lessons I learned in defeat. In a way, they seem to stay with you longer. Maybe it's because the pain and disappointment burn them into you.

1937 U.S. Open: Don't Count Your Chickens . . . I was a rookie in 1937, but I had already won and had begun to make a name for myself. When the Open came to Oakland Hills outside Detroit, I was listed as one of the favorites. That was pretty heady stuff for a twenty-five-year-old, but I tried to keep my mind on the job at hand. I figured that tough old bird of a course was going to give me all I could handle. And I was right.

I've always liked Oakland Hills: It's a hard test, but it's fair and the folks out in Detroit have always been good golf fans.

I played very well all week, and when I holed out my final putt on the last day, you'd think I was the most popular guy on the face of the earth. Folks swarmed around me, patting me on the back and congratulating me.

I finally made it to the locker room, and the newspaper guys were all over me trying to get their stories for the next day. Tommy Armour came by and congratulated me on winning the Open, but I wasn't so sure.

"Ralph Guldahl is still out there, and if he can make a couple birdies, he can still win it," I said.

Armour disagreed, saying that those closing holes were too tough. I hoped he was right. He wasn't.

When word reached the clubhouse that Ralph had made two birdies coming in to win, the place cleared out in a hurry. You could have fired off a gun and not hit anyone but me—and the way I was feeling, I kind of wished someone would.

Looking back, the loss was tough to take because it had looked for so long that I had won. It stayed with me for a long time, although I had come so close I was sure it was just a question of time before I eventually won the Open. The loss hurt, but it did teach me never to figure I had a tournament won until they handed me the trophy.

1939 U.S. Open: Know Where You Stand   The Open came to Philadelphia C.C. and, again, I was one of the favorites. I played very well and came to the last hole right in the thick of the fight. The problem was, I didn't know exactly where I stood. We didn't have the big scoreboards in those days, and I thought I needed to birdie the par-5 18th to tie Byron Nelson. In truth, I could have bogied the hole and still won. Hell, I could have played the hole with just a 6-iron and made a bogie.

Instead, I hit my drive into a fairway bunker. From there it was all downhill, and when I finally holed out, it was for a triple bogie eight. It was the lowest I ever felt, and it took me a long time to get over it. I lost ten pounds, my hair began to fall out in clumps, and the doctors told me I was headed for a nervous breakdown.

Today the players on tour know exactly where they stand, but my suggestion for everyone is to keep track of the match. There's no point in gambling when you don't need to. I learned that back in 1939, but it was a costly lesson.

1947 U.S. Open: Keep Your Composure   Lew Worsham and I tied at the end of regulation play and met for an 18-hole playoff the following day.

I didn't play especially well, but led by two going into the 16th hole. Chin ran in a long putt for a birdie there to cut the lead to one. On the 17th, my 8-iron approach ran through the green, into a collar of rough that had been matted down by the gallery. It was a tough shot, and the fact that Lew was standing nearby, breathing like an old steam engine, didn't make it any easier. I finally had to ask him to back off and give me some space. When he did, my shot came up 6 feet short, and I missed the putt. We came into 18 all even.

On 18, we both hit fine drives, and Lew's second shot ran through the green, stopping just short of the rough. His chip hit the cup, and the ball came to rest about 2 feet away.

My approach landed 25 feet past the hole, and I ran my first putt down to where I thought it was just inside Lew's ball. I was just about to tap in, when I heard Lew say, "Hey, what are you doing?"

"I'm putting out," I said.

"Are you sure you're away?" Lew asked. "I think I may be away."

According to the rules, in stroke play you are allowed to finish out regardless of who is away. But the referee, Ike Grainger, didn't answer me when I asked him about it. He simply measured. Lew's ball was 30 inches away, straight uphill—an easy putt. Mine was 30 1/2 inches, downhill with a left-to-right break. I missed. He made it. I had lost another Open.

Do I think Lew was using gamesmanship? Yes, but there was nothing illegal in what he did. The delay had broken my concentration and my composure, and I paid a high price for it.

The 1953 U.S. Open   Oakmont C.C. is one of the best tests in this country, and it was the place where I got one of my best lessons.

Going into the final round, Ben Hogan and I were neck and neck. Nowadays, the leaders are paired in the final rounds, which is how it should be, since you get to see what your opponent is doing, and you both play under identical conditions.

In 1953, however, the USGA did just about what they damn well pleased, and that included sending Ben out two hours before me. I was walking down the first fairway while Ben was playing the 10th hole. Not only did that give Ben a chance to play on greens that hadn't been spiked up, but it also gave him a chance to get in and post a score. That's a tremendous advantage.

Ben went on to win the Open that day, and I had to settle for another second-place finish. I would never again come that close in the Open.

My advice to you is to always get the earliest starting time you can. It gives you a chance to avoid spiked-up greens, it gives you a better chance to avoid getting behind slow players, and if you can post a good score, you give the other guys something to think about.

Winning at Match Play

I've always enjoyed match play because it gives you a chance to go face-to-face with your opponent and see what he's up to at all times. We used to play a lot more match play events on the tour than they do today, and I think it's a damn shame that we've gotten away from it because it's the game most people play at their clubs on the weekends and they can relate to it better than they can to 72 holes of medal play.

I've enjoyed a lot of success in match play and in playoffs. I always felt I had the edge because of my attitude toward competition. I'd like to share that with you before we get into some specific suggestions of how you can improve your chances in match play events.

I love to win. I always have. When I was a little kid, I always enjoyed the challenge of trying to win, no matter what I was doing.

I had an uncle, Ed Dudley, who I was very close to. We did

everything together—hunt, fish, play horseshoes and marbles—you name it, we did it, and I usually beat him at whatever we did. It drove him crazy.

One day when we were out fishing he had staked out the best pool in the stream. He was pulling in one beauty after another while I was being shut out. Finally, I'd had enough. I wandered off and found a big, old log and floated out on it until I could fish from his pool. I caught up in no time, but Unc was so mad at me he threatened to take a brush to my backside.

But as much as I love to win, I hate to lose even more. Call it pride or whatever you want, but it gets my goat to lose to someone I know I should be able to beat—and when I stepped onto the first tee, I always thought I was the man to beat.

Let me explain that last statement a bit. People often ask me who was the greatest golfer of all time, and my honest answer is that I don't know. The great players always find a way to win and I don't think it's right or fair to compare players from one era to those of another. But I will say this. I never felt there was a player I couldn't beat. If I felt otherwise, I had no business out on the tour. Did I think I could beat Ben Hogan? Hell yes, and I did it often enough. Nicklaus? Sure. And Jimmy Demaret, Arnold Palmer and anyone else you want to name.

Now that may sound boastful or arrogant, but I don't mean it to in any way. It's just the way I honestly feel, and the way I think you have to feel, if you are going to be a winner. I'm sure it's how Ben and Jack and the other top players over the years have felt.

The truth is, when it's time to compete, the players who win most often have a very strong attitude. They want to win and they don't like the fact that you are there to stop them. Off the course, I wouldn't hurt a flea, but when the starter says, "Play away," I don't care whom I'm up against, I want to beat them as badly as possible. If I have someone five down, I want to get it to six and then to seven. And if you don't think Bobby Jones and any of the other great players felt that way in their prime, you'd better think again.

I've always felt that it helps my game to play for a little something. People have a misconception that I'm a big-money player.

Well, I have played more than my share of matches with a lot of money on the line, but I play just as hard when it's a $5 nassau on the line as I do for a hundred times that. I just think it helps focus your attention that much more clearly. And believe me, it irks me just as much to lose $5 as it does to lose $50. It's not the money. It's a matter of pride.

I recall playing this fellow at The Homestead one day. He was a pretty good player, and I caught him on a strong day. He wound up nicking me for $20. When I paid him, he asked me to autograph the bill.

"What for?" I asked him.

"I want to frame it and put it in my office to prove that I actually beat you," he said.

"Well hell," I said, taking the $20 back from him. "In that case I'll give you a check."

After all, my pride may be more important than my money, but my mother didn't raise any idiots.

While I think it's a good idea to always play for a little something, I also believe you've got to be realistic and know what your choking point is. Lee Trevino is famous for saying that pressure is playing for $100 when you haven't got two quarters to rub together, but for a lot of people, the choking point is much lower than that.

I think betting on a round is a lot like going to the horse races: You should bet only what you figure you can afford to lose and still enjoy yourself. Of course, there is one difference: Whether you win or lose is all up to you, not a horse.

Gamesmanship: Avoiding the Needle   People think there's a lot of gamesmanship on the tour, but there really isn't. The fellows wouldn't put up with it. It's like cheating. If you cheat, you're hurting the game and taking food off everyone else's table.

One of the few run-ins I've had with gamesmanship involved Lloyd Mangrum. Lloyd was a very underrated player, but he was also one of the toughest men I've ever known.

I was paired with him one time, and every time I teed it up, he moved as close to me as he could and moved as I swung. I kept my mouth shut for as long as I could, but finally it got to be too much. With a huge gallery looking on, I stepped away from the ball.

"Lloyd," I said, looking him squarely in the eye and ready to mix it up with him if it came to that. "You've been trying to throw me off all day. All I want is a fair chance. Now give me a little room."

The gallery cheered and I remember one voice in particular saying, "Atta boy, Sam. He's been after you all day."

Lloyd never bothered me again. Not that day. Not ever.

There are all sorts of little things people say to throw off their opponent. Here are a few samples that, if you hear them, you can bet someone is trying to give you the needle. If that's the case, try to ignore the remark and concentrate on your own game—or just do what I do, which is tell the person to put his needle somewhere else.

- "It's unusual for someone with such a big loop in his backswing to hit the ball as well as you."
- "You know, I believe if you hit two big shots here, you can get home in two."
- "Damn, this is the slowest (or fastest) green on this course."

I've never believed much in giving the needle. It seems to me that it's more bother than it's worth, and your time and energy is better spent.

Reading Your Opponent   As I mentioned earlier, the beauty of match play is that you get to see what your opponent is up to at every moment. You don't have to rely on scoreboards or word of mouth, and most importantly, you can see whether he's brimming with confidence or being done in by the pressure.

One way to judge when the pressure is getting to your opponent is by watching his routine. Everyone has a pace of play and a routine that he follows, but when the noose starts to tighten, he falls out of his pace and routine. Instead of taking two practice swings, he may take three. He may hesitate over club selection. If he smokes, he may chain-smoke to try to calm his nerves. When you sense this, it's time to pour it on and turn up the pressure.

By the same token, if a player is rolling along on a streak, it helps to try to change the pace of play. Either play faster or slower than normal, but not so dramatically that you throw your game off. It's a small thing and perfectly legal, but it works often enough to make it worth trying.

Play for Pars   Bobby Jones never turned pro, and as a result he played much more match play competition at a high level than most other great players. While he was certainly capable of firing off strings of birdies, his one rule in match play was to play for pars. Nine times out of ten, par will be a good score. For middle to high handicap players, the same holds true for bogies.

And yet so often people come out of the gate firing for birdies and taking needless gambles. The result is that more often than not they find themselves behind the eight ball before the turn.

There is a time to gamble: if you are down in the match and running out of holes; if you sense an opening and a chance to demoralize the opposition; if you've got a realistic chance at a birdie early enough in the round to allow you to recover if the gamble fails.

Never Give Up   I know it's one of the oldest clichés in the game, but it's absolutely true. A match is never over until the final putt drops. I can't tell you how many times players have come back from being virtually closed out, only to beat the odds. There are few worse feelings than cruising along with a comfortable lead, only to watch helplessly as that lead begins to evaporate. When momentum turns in a golf match, it can turn in a big way. For that reason, a lot of very good players prefer not to be in the lead going into the final round. If you start a shot or two back, there's less pressure and you can freewheel a bit, trying to put some heat on the leader.

Assume the Worst   There's nothing more demoralizing than feeling that you've got a hole locked up, only to have your opponent run in a putt from another postal zone, or have your partner miss a gimme putt.

I think that it helps to be an optimist, but in golf you're better off if you don't anticipate good things happening. When they don't, it can set you off course in a second. I always assume that Murphy's Law was written by a golfer: If something can go wrong, it will.

Always Hole Out First   Just as in medal play, when the player who posts the first good score has an edge, I think that in match play it's a good idea to always play first and hole out first. It's just one more way of turning up the heat.

I believe that longer hitters always have an edge, but there are times when I'll deliberately lay up off the tee so I'll be away and hitting first. I figure that if I can cozy a shot in there close, there's just that much more pressure on my opponent.

The same holds true on the green. Rather than mark a short putt and wait, I'll take advantage of the option of finishing the hole. If I make the putt, my opponent has something to think about. If I miss, it may take just enough of the edge off so that he'll become careless.

Team Play   If you're like most people, when you play golf at your local club it's usually some form of team competition. Most folks get together and play a best-ball match for a little nassau. By and large, it's a nice way to socialize with friends for a few hours and get rid of some of the pressures that have built up during the week. All that's well and good, but I figure that if you're going to be out there anyway, you might as well give yourself every chance to win—which is why picking the right partner is so important.

Right off the bat, I think that everything else being equal, you want to try to team up with the best player because generally the better players don't give away enough strokes, while the higher handicappers don't get as many strokes as they deserve.

Almost as important—and in some cases, most important—is

The L.A. Open, 1950   The Legends of Golf, 1982

Memorable Tournaments
The Masters, 1952   The Masters, 1954

Top: 12th hole in 1952 with Ben Hogan
Bottom: Sam Snead after winning in 1954

finding a partner with whom you're compatible. Like any relationship, a team is going to go through some rocky moments, and it's a lot easier to get through them if you're paired with someone you like and respect.

It should go without saying that you should avoid arguing with, criticizing or second-guessing your partner. You just have to figure that he is doing the best he can, and if he makes a mistake, he probably feels at least as bad as you do, and probably worse.

Along those same lines, I don't think you should run around apologizing to your partner when things don't work out. After a while hearing someone tell you how sorry he is gets pretty old, and the chances are that if you just messed up, your partner is going to have to concentrate just that much harder to try to salvage the team's chances. It's hard to concentrate when someone is telling you how bad he feels all the time.

Horton Smith and Paul Runyan were a pretty formidable team back in their primes and they had a pretty good method of dealing with apologies. As they stood on the first tee, waiting to begin play, Horton would shake Paul's hand and apologize in advance for any mistakes he made. That was the last apology of the day from either of them—and that's a pretty good way of playing golf.

I think it's a good idea to pair with someone who hits the ball about the same distance as you do, because in team play you're able to give advice to your partner, and it's a lot easier to help someone with his club selection if you hit the ball about the same distance as your partner. This was the primary criterion I used to make the pairing when I captained the Ryder Cup teams in 1951, 1959 and 1969—and we were 2-0-1, so it must have some merit.

My next rule is to try to team with someone who has a different approach to the game. In other words, if you are a conservative player, it would be better for you to play with a bold, attacking golfer because you can give him or her a solid foundation to attack the course. It's a lot easier to try for birdies if you're confident your partner is going to protect par for you. Two teams that have been very successful in different eras with this approach have been Jack Nicklaus and Arnold Palmer and Lanny Wadkins and Larry Nelson. Neither Arnold nor Lanny ever met a pin placement he wouldn't attack, while both Larry and Jack are very methodical, conservative players who play the odds right down the line. But by pairing opposites, these two teams have been among the most successful in Ryder Cup play.

I think you should also avoid hotheads or people with negative attitudes. There's such a fine line between playing well and playing poorly, and this is such a mentally demanding game that listening to someone complain or watching him toss clubs all over the lot can be just enough to throw you off. The last thing you need is a partner who's going to get on your nerves. God knows, there's enough wear and tear on your nerves during a round as it is.

Somewhat along the same lines, I think it's important to team with someone who talks about the same amount you do. I always enjoyed playing with Ben Hogan because he went about his business and let me do the same. I think we both understood that and appreciated it in each other.

On the other hand, if Ben had been paired with a talkative player like Lee Trevino, it would have been hell on both of them.

One of the most interesting pairings I ever saw came one year in the Ryder Cup, when Lee Trevino was paired with Jerry Pate. I don't know how either one ever got a word in edgewise—and I can't imagine what it must have been like for their opponents.

Speaking of Trevino and Pate, there's an interesting story that gives you a little insight into team play.

Trevino asked to be teamed with Pate because he realized that in order for the Americans to win against a much improved European team, Pate had to win a majority of his points. He also realized that Pate, in his prime, had a tendency to try to do too much with a shot, especially under pressure.

Trevino took him aside before their match and told him there'd be times when he would pull the club for Pate to hit, and when he did, he didn't want Pate to do anything fancy, just put a good swing on the ball. Since Pate had so much respect for Trevino, he agreed to give it a try, and he played some of his finest golf in those matches.

Another example of outstanding teamwork occurred in the 1987 Ryder Cup matches at Muirfield Village in Ohio. The Americans had lost the 1985 matches in England, and we were facing an even stronger European team determined to not only defend the title, but also to beat us on our own soil for the first time in history. Seve Ballesteros, the top European player, realized that the play of his fellow Spaniard, Jose-Maria Olazabal, was going to be crucial to Europe's chances for success. He asked Captain Tony Jacklin to pair him with the younger and less experienced Olazabal, who greatly admired and respected Seve.

The pairing was magical. Seve counseled and settled the naturally nervous Olazabal, and they gave the Americans all they could handle. The point of these stories is that in team play, success often hinges on your knowledge of your partner, and the respect you have for his abilities.

There are two other points about picking a partner that seem pretty obvious, but are worth mentioning.

First, if you are playing away from home, it's a good idea to try to hook up with a member. Believe me, there is such a thing as local knowledge in this game, and a lot of times it's enough to make the difference between winning and losing.

I'll give you a good example of how local knowledge can help, and how not having it can cost you a tournament.

I imagine I know Augusta National about as well as any man alive, but every time I play it I learn some new little quirk I hadn't noticed before. Since I played a lot of my practice rounds with my nephew, J.C., I would naturally pass along little bits of local knowledge as they came to me.

I've always thought J.C. had the game to win at Augusta because he's a long hitter and he can get it going with his putter. In 1973 he had his best chance. He came into the par-3 12th hole right in the thick of things. I was watching on television as he stood on the tee, trying to gauge what the wind was doing.

Now even on a calm day the 12th is a bear because the green is so small and the penalties for missing it are so severe. Rae's Creek just seems to sit there and say, "C'mon boy, I dare you to shoot at the pin." But it's rarely calm there, and when the wind blows, it comes shooting down that valley, gets up in those pines and starts swirling around. That means if you check one group of trees, the wind looks as if it's coming from one direction, but another set of trees makes it seem as if it's coming from just the opposite. And on top of that, the flag might be blowing from a third direction—or it might just hang there, limp as an old dishrag.

It's not unusual to stand on the tee and feel the wind quartering off your left shoulder, which should be a helping wind. That's the trick because the wind is coming down the valley and swinging around behind you. Down by the green, the wind is actually against you. But J.C. didn't know that, and as I sat there I just hoped that somehow he'd pull the right club. Instead, he got confused by the swirling winds, pulled the wrong club and shot his way out of a green jacket with a double-bogie. He didn't hit the wrong shot, he just got tricked by the old girl.

My other rule—and this is a hard and fast one—is never bet with your partner. This game is tough enough without pulling against a guy on one bet whom you should be pulling for on another. As soon as I hear my opponents putting a little something down on the side, I ask if they'd like to raise the stakes on the team bet. After all, a golden opportunity like that doesn't come along every day. It's like money in the bank.

The last area in teamwork that I'd like to talk about is helping your partner. You have to walk a fine line here because some people like to get all the help they can, while others prefer to be left pretty much alone. One reason I teamed so well with Gardner Dickinson was that we both liked to get and give about the same amount of advice, and we respected each other enough to take the advice that was offered.

As I said before, if you are paired with a player who hits the ball about the same distance as you, it makes it a lot easier to help with club selection. But where life really gets complicated is on the greens because some players are very aggressive putters while others like to lag the ball up to the hole. Since the speed of a putt determines how much effect the grain and the break will have on the ball, it makes it tough for an aggressive putter to help read a putt for a more conservative putter.

A good example of this was the 1988 World Cup at Royal Melbourne Golf Club in Melbourne, Australia. Doc Middlecoff and I represented America in the World Cup on this course back in 1959, and I was playing well enough to set the course record. It's one of the best courses you'll ever see, but those greens are mighty tough to handle.

Naturally, I was curious to see how the course looked after all these years, so I turned on the World Cup. Ben Crenshaw and Mark McCumber were paired for the United States and I noticed that Mark was relying on Ben for a lot of help in reading putts.

Now on the face of it, you couldn't ask for a better person than Ben Crenshaw to read putts for you. I imagine he's as good a putter as ever lived. But the catch is that he's very much a lag putter, while Mark is very aggressive. The break Ben would read for Mark isn't necessarily the break the putt would take because Mark hits his putts more firmly than Ben.

Sure enough, while the Americans won, and Ben won the individual title, it took a while before Ben and Mark could get in sync when it came time to read putts. It's just one of the factors that make team play so fascinating.

The lesson is that if you're going to help your partner read his putts, you'd better have a pretty good idea how hard he plans to hit it.

There are two rules that I go by when I'm on the green. The first is that I think a team should always let the player with the easiest putt go first. The second is that you should never attack a putt that you don't need. Let me explain.

How often have you been in a situation where your partner has a reasonable putt for a birdie—say something under 10 feet—and you have a shorter putt for a par? Conventional wisdom is that you should try to make the par before letting your partner try for his birdie, but I disagree. If you miss the par putt, you've turned up the pressure on your partner, who now has to worry about par and can't take an aggressive run at a birdie. As I said earlier, you want to do everything you can to take the pressure off your team and yourself, and put as much heat as you can on your opponents.

I suggest that in this situation you let your partner try his birdie putt first. If he makes it, you're home free. If he misses, the chances are he's not going to miss by much, and you've still got two putts left for par.

As far as gunning at putts you don't need, this comes under the category of keeping your ego in check. It's only natural to want to run up as many birdies as possible. Hell, posting a good number is what this game is all about. But when you have a partner, you have to do what's best for the team. I've been in plenty of situations where my partner has a putt for a birdie, but only needs a par to win the hole. When that's the case, I remind him of an old saying we have back home in Virginia: "The Good Lord hates a coward, but he's not real fond of a fool, either."

Some Memorable Tournaments
Learning from Winning

*T*he **1942 PGA Championship: Watch Your Opponent** The PGA Championship was a match play event until 1958, and I always enjoyed it for that reason. Of course, winning it three times didn't hurt, either.

This was a big tournament for me. I had enlisted in the Navy, and with the war on, none of us knew when we'd be back on tour—or if we would, for that matter.

I faced Jim Turnesa in the 36-hole final at Seaview C.C. outside Atlantic City. Jim was a hell of a player. He had beaten Ben Hogan, Byron Nelson and Dutch Harrison on his way to the finals. Our match was tight, and we were dead even through 27 holes. I kept a close eye on Jim, and he wasn't showing any signs of cracking under the pressure. That is, he didn't show any signs until the 10th hole.

Some players walk faster under pressure. Some chain-smoke. Others fidget or get out of their routine. Still others talk more or become very quiet. In Jim's case, I noticed that he changed the way he waggled his club before he played. All day long he had taken two smooth waggles. On the 10th, he made four short, jerky waggles. I knew I had him. Sure enough, he hooked his tee ball into the woods. His second shot hit another tree, and I won the hole with a four. I wound up winning my first Major, 2&1.

Since most amateurs play weekend matches, often against the same guys, I'd suggest you make it a point of getting to know your opponent's mannerisms. They'll give you a clue when it's time to turn up the heat and when it's time to lay low.

1946 British Open   I never played in many British Opens. In fact, I played in only three—1937, '46 and '62. The main reason was financial. You had to win the championship to even come close to making your expenses back. But in 1946 the people from Wilson asked if I'd go over to help promote Wilson equipment, and since they had always been good to me, I agreed to go.

I got myself in hot water right off the bat. As the train pulled into St. Andrews early in the evening, I happened to be looking out the window and saw what I thought looked like an old golf course.

"Say, that looks as if it might have been a golf course that's gone to seed," I mentioned to the fellow next to me.

"Why, sir, that's the Old Course at St. Andrews," he said.

As you can imagine, the newspapers had a field day with that one. You'd think I had insulted the Queen.

I was a 10–1 favorite, but from the first I had a tough time adjusting to the conditions. The weather would change in the blink of an eye. In the final round it was so cold I wore my pajamas under my regular clothes just to keep warm. The small ball took some getting used to, and it took me three tries before I found a caddie I could live with.

I opened up with a 71, followed with a 70, and my third-round 74 was good enough to keep me toe-to-toe with South Africa's Bobby Locke, at 7–1 the pre-tournament favorite, and my old traveling companion, Johnny Bulla, who had helped persuade me to enter the championship.

I thought I had things pretty well in hand in the final round, until the 530-yard, par-5 5th hole jumped up and bit me. The wind was howling from left to right, and I tried to draw the ball into it. The shot got away from me and wound up in the Hell bunker on the 14th hole. I knocked it out with a 3-iron, but the ball ran across the 5th fairway and into the Whins—a patch of thick, prickly gorse. The stuff was so mean that the ball just hung up in it, about a foot off the ground. If that wasn't bad enough, the wind rocked the gorse back and forth, to and fro.

I didn't know what to do. I could have taken a drop, but I figured that if I could time it just right, I could take a baseball swing with a 6-iron and move the ball down the fairway. I took my time, trying to match up my swing with the swaying gorse. Wham! That ball came out of there like a quail flushed by a hound. The ball ran into a bunker short of the green.

Now I really was in a jam. I had to carry the ball some 75 yards, but the face of the bunker was so steep that I was stymied. I needed an 9-iron to reach the green, but I needed the loft of a wedge to clear the face of the bunker. If it had been an earlier round, I might have just pitched safely back into the fairway, but I was running out of holes. I decided to gamble.

I always felt comfortable with a 9-iron in my hand, so that's what I grabbed. I opened the face up, played the ball forward in my stance and swung down sharply on the ball with a very wristy action. She came out of there like a rocket, and two putts later I came away with one of the few bogies I was ever happy to make. But anytime you have to invent two shots on a hole, bogie is a pretty good score.

As I mentioned a bit earlier, the caddies over there were beauties. After the award ceremony, my caddie asked if he could keep the ball I had won with. He said he would cherish it all his life. I found out that he went down to the nearest pub and sold it before the sun had gone down.

The 1950 Los Angeles Open: Concentrate on Your Work   The Los Angeles Open has always been one of the big events on the tour. In the early days Wilson would give you a bonus if you won it, which I always figured was a pretty good indication of how important a tournament really was.

Riviera is a great golf course, although it used to be a lot tougher because there was a barranca that ran through the place and was hell to pay if you hit into it.

In 1950 the tournament took on added meaning. It was the first time Ben Hogan would play competitively since the auto accident that damn near killed him. Nobody was sure how Ben would do, although all the guys were pulling for the little man. We hoped he'd be able to finish, but we should have known that Ben wouldn't have showed up just to play four rounds.

Ben played awfully well, and when rain washed out Sunday's round, it gave him a chance to rest his legs. He came back firing, with 69s in the third and fourth rounds. When he posted his score, there was only one person on the course who could catch him, and I needed to birdie two of the last four holes to do it. And those holes are killers.

I got pars on 15 and 16, birdied 17 by draining a 14-footer and then faced a 15-footer on 18 for a tie.

The final green at Riviera sits in a sort of natural bowl. The hillside rises sharply behind the green, and on that day there were hundreds, maybe thousands of people jammed in there. As I stood over my putt, I heard a big crash, and people scrambled to see what had happened.

As it turned out, a man had been sitting in a tree when a limb collapsed beneath him. He fell down through some vines and bushes. There was such an uproar that I had to back away from my putt and gather myself.

As I waited, I heard the guy yell, "Don't worry, Sam. I'm all right."

To be real honest, his safety wasn't my biggest concern. I just tried to get comfortable over the ball, find the line again and put a good stroke on the ball. I did, and Ben and I were tied.

The playoff wasn't held until the following week because the tournament had been delayed so often by rain and we were committed to play in Bing Crosby's tournament. When we did play off, it really wasn't much of a match. I shot a one-over-par 72 and Ben shot a 76. I won $2,600 and Ben got $1,900. We both split the gate receipts, which came to about $1,000 each.

The big—and good—news was that Ben was back. I went on and won ten tournaments that year and was also the leading money winner. Ben was named player of the year. I never understood the logic behind that, but then again it's not always a logical game.

The 1982 Legends of Golf: Pouring It On   My idea of a perfect match is beating someone, 10&8. I never understood someone who didn't want to beat his opponent too badly. When I'm playing someone, I just want to pound him into the turf. Then we can have a nice friendly few holes. Some folks may not understand that, but I believe that's how you have to think in order to win.

I like the story that Claude Harmon told me about the advice Ben Hogan gave him just before the 1959 U.S. Open at Winged Foot, where Claude was the pro.

"Claude," Ben said, "your problem is that you play 'happy golf.' You just want to be friendly with everyone. At Winged Foot this year, you just keep your head down, don't visit with anyone during the round and go about your business."

Well, Claude did as he was told, but it damn near killed him. He'd make that walk between the 9th green and the 10th tee looking at his feet. All his members would be saying "Hi," and "Good Luck" and Claude just kept walking. He finished third, two shots behind Billy Casper, who putted like a demon. Ben had proven his point, but I'm not sure how well it set with all Claude's members.

At the 1982 Legends I was teamed with Don January, who is seventeen years younger than I and had just become eligible to play in the tournament. You might say we teamed pretty well in the 54-hole event. I made fourteen birdies. Don made thirteen. We never bogied a par 3, playing them in ten under par. We were nine under on the par 4s and eight under on the par 5s.

We got off to a smooth start, leading by one shot after the opening round, eight after the second and finally wound up cutting the field by twelve shots.

As we were coming down the stretch, I birdied 15 and 16. At that point Don turned to me and asked, "Man, how much do you want to win by, Sam?"

"You never know," I replied. "Those folks up there might be cheating."

The point is that you can never let up. The more you can win by, the more doubts you put in the other players' minds the next time out. Besides, people are paying good money to watch us play. They don't want to see a bunch of guys laying up, right?

Equipment
Buying a Better Game

*A*s I've said a thousand times, you can't go into a shop and buy a good golf game. No matter how much God-given talent you might have, you're only going to get as much out of the game as you put into it. That's not to say you can't place a down payment on a better game by investing in some equipment that is suited, not only to your game, but also to the course you're playing.

I've played in thousands of pro-ams and outings over the years, and I'll be very honest and tell you that most people have equipment that is either such junk to begin with, or so poorly suited to their needs, that even if a genie popped out of a bottle, tapped them on the shoulder and gave them the most beautiful swing of all time, they still couldn't break their leg, much less par.

One of the biggest advantages the guys on tour have today is that equipment is so much better, and they have access to all the latest

139

technology. As a result, they are very picky about getting just the right shafts, grips, swingweights, lies and loft, and all the rest. If the best players in the world are that careful, I've never understood why the average Joe thinks he can walk in a shop or store, pick up a set off the rack and expect to change his game overnight.

In this section I'd like to give you some guidelines for putting together a combination of clubs and balls that will fit you and go a long way toward cutting some strokes off your score.

Be Realistic   It's only human nature that the weekend golfer looks to the touring pros and believes that if he could just play the same equipment, he could lower his scores. I can't really complain about that, since that belief has been very good to both me and the Wilson Sporting Goods Company over the years.

In a way, they're right. Our clubs are matched to our body types and swings, but we're able to select the club specifications we need because we've experimented and fine-tuned our equipment over the years.

Too often people hear that a fellow plays with a certain kind of club or shaft or ball, and they think that's the secret for them. The truth is, most people aren't strong enough and can't generate enough clubhead speed to use the same equipment as the pros. But that's not to say you shouldn't experiment a little or be as demanding as we are about the tools of the trade.

The rules of golf say that you can carry fourteen clubs, but they don't say which fourteen, and that doesn't mean that you can't have a few extras in your locker.

Most standard sets are made up of 2- through 9-irons, a pitching wedge and sand wedge, a putter, driver, 3-wood and 4-wood. What I do—and what a lot of better players do—is alternate between a 4-wood and 1-iron, depending on the course and the wind conditions.

A 1-iron and 4-wood will hit the ball about the same distance, but you can hit the 1-iron lower than a 4-wood because the wood has more weight along the sole of the club, which helps get the ball into the air. This makes a 1-iron a good club to have if you are playing in very windy conditions. However, if you are playing a course that requires high, soft approach shots, such as Augusta National, you'll see a lot of the boys go with a 4-wood rather than try to force additional height out of their 1-iron.

Now that's just one example of how course conditions dictate which clubs should be in your bag. But before you run out and buy a 1-iron, you should understand that it's a very difficult club to hit, and most folks would be better off sticking with a 4-wood. In fact, I'd go so far as to suggest that the vast majority of golfers would be doing themselves a big favor by dropping their 2-irons and 3-irons and replacing them with a 5-wood and a 6-wood. Fairway woods such as these are more forgiving than long irons, and easier for most people to hit because you sweep the ball off the turf, rather than hitting down on it as you do with an iron.

The other advantage fairway woods offer most golfers is that they are much better for hitting the ball out of the rough. When you try to hit an iron—especially a long iron—from the rough, you must guard against the high grass tangling around the hosel of the club, which allows the blade to close too quickly and results in a low, duck hook. A wood's design prevents this from happening, and the additional weight along the sole helps lift the ball into the air more easily.

The best evidence to support my case for fairway woods is a look at the clubs the pros use in tournaments like the U.S. Open, where the USGA makes sure there's plenty of deep rough protecting the landing areas. More than any other tournament, the Open forces players to drop their 1-irons and maybe even their 2-irons and go to fairway woods.

Add a Third Wedge   Another development in recent years has been the use of a 60-degree wedge. Tom Kite was the first player on tour to use one, and he used it so effectively that a number of the other pros put one in their bag. It wasn't long before the word got out and a number of manufacturers began selling them.

I think these are excellent clubs for most golfers, especially if you play on a course that has greens protected by mounds and severe rough. A 60-degree wedge allows you to hit high, soft, floating lob shots. You must guard against trying to hit the ball too far, however, because the harder you swing, the higher the ball will go. It will take some practice to get a feel for how high and how far you can hit the ball with this club, but it's a worthwhile investment.

When Tom started using a 60-degree wedge, I asked him what club he dropped from his set to stay within the fourteen-club limit. His answer will give you some idea just how sophisticated today's players are when it comes to their equipment.

Tom explained that, rather than drop a club, he slightly altered the lofts of his clubs so that there wasn't as much difference between his irons as there would be in a traditional set. Now that is really fine-tuning your equipment, and while it's not realistic to expect many of you to go that far, I'd like to suggest that you keep a record of which clubs you hit over the course of five or so rounds. This will give you an idea which clubs you use most often, and which club you can afford to replace with a third wedge.

Buying Your Clubs

Golf has changed a lot over the years, and one of the biggest changes has been in the way people buy equipment. Years ago about the only place you could get equipment was a pro shop or sporting goods store. Today there are huge golf retailers selling volumes of equipment that would have been unthinkable not so very long ago. You can even order clubs through the mail.

Now I don't want to put the knock on anybody, but I will just say that I wouldn't buy a car without giving it a test drive, and the same holds true for buying a set of clubs. If you are dealing with a reputable professional, he'll let you go out and hit a bucket of balls with a club to make sure it feels good to you. The only exception might be a sand wedge, which becomes worn merchandise after a few swipes in the sand.

The other advantage to buying clubs through a professional is that, if he is a good, smart professional, he'll go out of his way to make sure that the clubs are properly fitted to your build and your swing. Again, it's like any other business. You want to satisfy your customers to make sure they keep coming back.

The Game Today

Top: David Frost, Greg Norman, Isao Aoki, Bernhard Langer
Bottom: Nick Faldo, Sandy Lyle, Seve Ballesteros

Right here is a good spot to give you a checklist of the things you should look for when buying a set of clubs—and remember, clubs are an investment you have to live with for a long time, so don't rush into any decisions.

Eye Appeal   My first consideration is how a club looks to me. Everyone has individual likes and dislikes, but I think that if a club doesn't look right sitting there behind the ball, it's hard to work up a lot of confidence in either the club or the shot you're trying to play. The best example I can give you dates back to 1937 and a driver that I got from Henry Picard.

I was having a terrible time driving the ball. I couldn't find a driver I liked and I couldn't find a fairway with a road map. Henry came along with one of his drivers and suggested I give it a try. It was love at first sight, and I used it until 1970, when she finally wore out completely. On more than one occasion, I'd hit a drive and the head would go rocketing down the fairway with Old Sam in hot pursuit. The galleries got a kick out of seeing me racing after that clubhead, but losing it would have been like losing my right arm.

Cast vs. Forged Irons   Years ago the majority of the irons looked pretty much the same. The so-called traditional blade was forged and then ground by craftsmen into a specific design. On tour, individual players would have certain things that they liked or didn't like in a blade, and that became known as their personal "grind." Eventually, the best of these qualities made their way into the sets of the major manufacturers and were sold in shops.

Now there are more different kinds of irons out there than you can shake a stick at. The biggest change has been in what are called cast clubs, popularized by Ping irons and now widely copied by other companies.

These clubs are more forgiving of off-center hits than traditional blades because the weight is distributed around more of the clubhead.

This helps the higher handicapper because it minimizes his misses, but for the better player, I'm not sure they are such a good bet. In the times I've tried them, I don't believe that they allow you to put fade or draw spin on the ball.

I think what it comes down to for you is an honest assessment of your game and needs. If you are a pretty fair ball striker, then a traditional blade may give you a little more shotmaking ability. If you need the help, then one of these so-called self-correcting clubs might be worth a try. Either way, it's something to talk over with your pro before making any decisions.

Metal Woods   Perhaps the biggest revolution in the game is the increased popularity of metal woods. Actually, they aren't really all that new. Years ago they were widely used at driving ranges because they held up better under the punishment.

Of course, those old metal woods look like something out of the Stone Age compared with the clubs being made today. I never thought I'd see the day when I'd give up my old persimmon drivers, but I've convinced metal woods have a lot of merit, and I'll explain why.

For starters, metal woods are a lot more durable than traditional woods, which could be affected by changes in temperature as well as by moisture. You also have the luxury of a variety and a consistency of lofts in metal clubs.

I think the biggest advantage to metal clubs is that they are designed to be more forgiving when you hit the ball out off the toe or heel. As a result, your misses tend to be straighter, and that gives you just a little greater margin for error. And since they are lighter, you can produce greater combined speed and power.

Metal woods aren't for everyone. I know a lot of players who grew up playing with those beautiful, old wooden clubheads and can't get used to either the look or feel of metal. In a sense, there's a big part of me that's still in that camp. I always have my eye open for a wooden driver that's made just right, but I'm not going to shut the door on something new, just because it's different. A fellow needs every edge he can get these days.

Try a 2-Wood   I'm going to say something right here and now that a lot of you won't want to hear, won't believe, or will just go ahead and ignore. I'd say at least 50 percent of the people who read this book—who read any golf book for that matter—would be better off putting their driver in the closet and trying a 2-wood.

Why? For starters, the 2-wood has more loft and just looks easier to hit. So often I see players with an old, straight-faced, 9- or 10-degree lofted driver, struggling to help the ball into the air. It's useless, and the fact that the club has so little loft also makes it very unforgiving when you mishit the ball.

Recently some studies were done that proved that unless you can generate about as much clubhead speed as a professional, you can't get the maximum benefit from a driver. However, by using a 2-wood— or in some cases a 3-wood—from the tee, you'll be able to drive the ball higher, straighter and farther. That's a lot of benefits for the small price of swallowing a little bit of ego.

Find the Correct Shafts   One of the biggest improvements in equipment in the last decade has been the development of shafts that can be closely matched to a player's needs.

Of course, when I started to play, we used hickory shafts. They were different each day because they were so easily affected by the weather. You could hit the ball a long way, but you couldn't practice nearly as much as you could with metal because they wouldn't hold up to the punishment. They also had a tremendous amount of torque, which forced you to wait on the shot so the clubhead could square up. That took a lot of timing.

Metal shafts were a revolution, and that's true of the shafts today. They are available in a variety of types of metal, as well as in graphite and other space age materials. Through the use of computers and testing, companies have developed patterns of steps in the shafts that not only finely tune the stiffness of the shaft, but also the so-called kick point—the point on the shafts where it flexes and then kicks back as the clubhead reaches impact. Depending on the kick point and the shaft flex, a player can vary the height he hits his average shot. In the past, you had to do this by changing your swing.

It used to be that shafts came in three flexes—stiff, regular and flexible. Now they come in numerous variations within those ranges. I've always used stiff shafts, but I know a lot of the guys vary their shaft flexes through the set, with the longer clubs having the stiffer shafts.

My advice to you is to experiment with a variety of shafts, under the supervision of a knowledgeable professional. The ideal is the shaft that gives you the best feel, distance and control. But be prepared to spend enough time. The right shaft is the most important element in building a club that's right for you.

Find the Correct Grip   Your hands are the only parts of your body that come in contact with the club during the swing, so it only stands to reason that you want to have grips that give you both the best feel and control.

There are two basic concerns when having grips placed on your clubs: size and material. I played with leather grips for much of my career, but switched when good rubber grips were developed. I liked the way they felt, and they didn't require nearly as much upkeep as leather, which must continually be cleaned and softened or the grips will become slick and hard. A number of good players, particularly those from the warmer parts of the country, favored cord grips— rubber grips with rough, cotton laced through the grip. They felt it gave them more control when their hands began to sweat. I felt the early cord grips were too harsh and punishing on my hands, and I didn't like the feel. Today's cord grips, however, are softer and are a good compromise. Again, as in so much of this game, I think you have to experiment and find what grip feels best to you.

Feel will also determine how thick the grips on your clubs should be. As a general rule, you want the tips of the fingers on your left hand to just barely touch the palm of your left hand when you grip the club. A grip that is too thin will promote a quick release of the club at impact, while grips that are too thick will tend to delay your release.

I think it's worth your while to try a variety of different-sized grips and types of grips. Finding the combination that's most comfortable and gives you the most feel can make a world of difference.

Check Your Lofts and Lies   Even once you've found a set of clubs that have the correct grips and shafts for your game, you're not quite finished. People often overlook the lies and lofts of their clubs, both when they first get the set and after they've played with them for a while.

Clubmakers operate from a fairly standard series of lofts that are consistent throughout the industry. A Wilson 5-iron will have the same loft as a Spalding 5-iron and so on, at least in theory. In reality, human error occasionally enters the picture and you might not always get the correct lofts throughout the set. For that reason, it's a good idea to have the lofts checked before you buy a new set. If they're off, it's a lot easier—and cheaper—to get them fixed before you've taken them out the door. It's also a good idea to have your lofts checked at least once a year if you play a lot of golf. You may find that a club or two that you hit fairly often may need to be corrected. It's an easy and inexpensive process.

Clubs also come with fairly standard lies. That is, the average set of clubs is designed so that the golfer of average size, height and swing shape can pick up a set off the rack and have the soles of the clubs rest squarely on the ground.

Notice that I stressed "average." If you are taller or shorter than average, or have a flatter or more upright swing, you should have clubs whose lies are altered to fit your build and swing. For example, a tall player with an upright swing should have clubs that are a degree or two upright, while a shorter or heavier player with a flatter swing needs his clubs built a degree or two flat.

Clubs with lies that are incorrect not only restrict your ability to make solid contact, but they also make it difficult to aim the club properly. Again, this is an easy matter to test, and while it may take a little longer to get a set that is properly fitted, it's worth the wait to get a set that's right the first time.

Play the "Right" Ball   As most folks know, I've been with Wilson Sporting Goods for most of my career, and I've like to think it's been a good relationship for everyone concerned. And while I think Wilson makes some damn good balls, when I say the "right" ball, I mean the type of ball that's best for you.

For most players, a two-piece, synthetic covered ball is the one they should be playing, for the simple reason that you can't cut up those little beauties. A wound balata-covered ball will spin more, that's true. And that's why most of the boys on tour play them. But the average Joe can't put that much spin on the ball to begin with, so why not think in terms of dollars and cents instead of ego. After all, the players on the tours don't have to pay for the balls they use, but you do.

Balls, like so much else in the field of equipment, have improved dramatically. Why, it used to be that you'd give your eyeteeth for a round one. Now they have balls that help you hit the ball higher, and others to help you hit it lower. The new balls are somewhat self-correcting, which is good for the weekend player who might be a little wild, but makes it a little more difficult to work the ball left or right. It's all a trade-off, but I do believe most folks would be better off with a ball that will help them hit straighter shots than they would with a ball that's going to encourage them to try shots they shouldn't even be dreaming about in the first place.

Get a Good Sand Wedge   When Gene Sarazen invented the sand wedge years ago, he made this game a whole lot easier for a whole lot more people. From the first time the old Scotsmen came face-to-face with a bunker, golfers have been scared to death of the sand. Gene's club made the sand shot easier, but most people don't have a club that will help them, and as a result it still terrifies players to this day.

What Sarazen figured out was that if you made the trailing edge of the flange lower than the leading edge, you created "bounce," which allowed the club to glide through the sand and under the ball. The sand throws the ball out, and if played properly, the clubhead never comes in contact with the ball, making the sand shot one with a large margin for error.

The problem is that most people need a club with more bounce than the one they have, usually for one of two reasons. First, few people take the time to go to their pro for a lesson in sand play, or even bother to ask whether they've got a sand club with enough bounce to fit their abilities. Or else, in order to use their sand wedge from the fairway, they have a wedge with so little bounce that it's not worth the powder to blow it across the street.

This is particularly true if you play down south or in other areas where courses have very fine, powdery sand. You need a club with a decent amount of loft, weight and bounce to get through the sand. Up north, where the sand is coarser and firmer, you can get away with a thinner flange and less bounce—but experience tells me that nine times out of ten, even up north, people are trying to make do with a club that might be fine for a touring pro, but not for most players.

A good sand wedge, a driver and a putter are the three most important clubs for scoring. Yet while most folks spend a lot of time trying drivers and putters, they'll usually take whatever wedge is on sale at the moment. That's not money well spent, not in my book.

Finding the Right Putter   I suppose that of all the clubs, the putter is the most fickle and difficult to find. I know very few players who stick with one type of putter—let alone one putter—throughout their career.

I do believe, however, that the first rule is to find a putter that looks and feels good to you, since that will instill a measure of confidence. It's a funny thing, I can go down a rack of putters that look identical, but I might be able to find only one or two that I'd even bother taking to the putting green for a trial run. That's one reason you should never get rid of a putter that looks and feels right. Eventually it will look good to you again, so just put her away in a locker or closet until it's time to give her another chance.

I do have a couple of specific thoughts about putters. First, I think that a center-shafted putter is best because it's a little more forgiving of putts hit away from the sweet spot. Second, it's easier to aim than a blade with its hosel toward the heel.

I also think that one reason slightly bigger putters have become popular is that they are easier to aim. People often criticized Jack Nicklaus for taking so much time over a putt, and I think one reason is that the blade on his old George Low Wizard was so small it just took him a long time to aim the putter. Of course, I did notice that Jack was beating most of the people who were complaining, and that might have had something to do with all the talk.

Some Memorable Tournaments
Two Lessons from Augusta

*A*ugusta National and the Masters has always had a special spot in my heart. The folks there always treated me very well, and going there in April, with all the flowers and shrubs in bloom, always meant that spring had arrived back home.

Of course, it didn't hurt any that I have such fond memories of the place. I won in 1949, '52 and '54, finished second twice and had fourteen top 10 finishes in all.

My last year as an active competitor was 1983. The course had just gotten too long for me, and I didn't want to take up one of the younger guys' spots. Now I go there to play in the Par 3 tournament and serve as one of the honorary starters, along with Byron Nelson and Gene Sarazen. And, of course, I look forward to seeing all the fellows at the champion's dinner.

I think Augusta is one of the fairest courses on the tour. It rewards power and aggressiveness, especially on the par 5s. You have to be accurate with your approaches, and you'd better be able to putt that week or you're in for a short stay.

To me, the proof of a tournament's worth is in the list of winners it produces. When you look at the guys who have won at Augusta, you don't see many flukes or so-called One-Shot Johnnys on the list.

The 1952 Masters: Just Keep Plugging Away   Coming into the tournament, the writers had made Ben and me co-favorites, and with good reason. From the time I won in 1949 until 1956, Ben and I either won or finished second each year except 1950, when Jimmy Demaret edged Jim Ferrier.

For three rounds, we made them look pretty good. We were tied at 214 going into the last round, and I went out an hour ahead of Ben—a plus for me. It was smooth sailing until the 155-yard, par-3 12th—one of the toughest holes in golf.

You begin with a very narrow green, guarded by bunkers and Rae's Creek, which winds down in front of the green. To make matters worse, the wind dives and swirls through the tall pines, making club selection extremely difficult.

With the pin tucked on the right side of the green, I picked a 6-iron and hit it right on the nose. But just as the ball took off, a gust of wind came up and the ball dove like a bird that had just been hit with a 12-gauge. It fell into the bank on the far side of the creek, then ever so slowly, began trickling back down into the water.

I didn't have a play, so I was forced to take a drop on the far side of the water. To make matters worse, the ball settled into some thick, wet grass. There was no way I could put any spin on the ball, and as it turned out, my shot barely cleared the creek and left me with a 20-foot chip from a lie that forced me to stand with my left foot well above my right.

I took out my 8-iron and popped right down on the back of the ball. I caught it clean and then looked on in amazement as it wobbled toward the hole, a big glob of mud stuck to the side. It looked like a ball you'd buy in a joke shop, and believe me, I had a smile on my face when that little beauty dove into the hole for a lifesaving bogie.

After that scare, I went on to finish with an even par 72, to win with a 286. Jackie Burke was second with 290 and Ben soared to a 79.

1954 Masters: Head-to-Head with Hogan   I would have to say that of all my wins, this one might have been the sweetest. To face Ben in a playoff for the Masters is what competition is all about.

Going into the back nine an amateur, Billy Joe Patton, had a very good chance to win. His first mistake was going for the green on 13. He put it in the creek, then did the same thing on 15 to set the stage for Monday's 18-hole playoff between Ben and me. One of the biggest galleries I've ever seen turned out to watch, and I think they got a pretty good show. I still remember it shot for shot.

On the first tee I asked Ben if he wanted to split the purse, which was pretty common in those days. Ben took a couple tight drags on his cigarette and said, "Let's play." And so we did.

We both made the turn with one-under-par 35s and then, as is so often the case at Augusta's back nine, the game was on. I chipped in from 65 feet on 10 to take the lead, but gave it back with a bogie on 12. On 13, I hit a big drive around the corner and reached the green with a crisp 3-iron. Ben laid up short of the water, and I won the hole with a birdie. We matched each other with pars and birdies on 14 and 15.

On the par-3 16th, I hit it to 25 feet, and Ben put his tee shot inside me, about 18 feet away. As I looked over my putt, I noticed that Ben seemed nervous. He was really dragging away on his cigarette, and with a one-shot lead, I decided to take a real run at my putt, hoping to turn up the heat on the Hawk. My putt ended up a foot past the hole, and I sat back to see what Ben would do.

Ben's nerves very rarely got to him, but he hit one of the worst putts I've ever seen him hit. His putter hit behind the ball, and the ball was 5 feet short. When he missed from there, I had a two-shot lead and a big boost in my confidence.

On 17, I cracked a big drive, but when I reached the ball, I noticed that it was sitting on top of an old, dried-out divot. If I had grounded my club, the ball would have moved and I would have taken a penalty. I couldn't believe I had gotten such a bad break. I didn't have a clue how to play the shot, so I just grabbed a 6-iron and hit the ball perfectly. It ended up 40 feet from the hole, and it was on to 18, my lead still intact.

On 18, I put my 3-iron second shot in the right bunker, blasted out and took two putts for a bogie that gave me the win, 70–71.

As I've said, it's always great to win, but when you can go head-to-head with a player like Ben Hogan, it just makes it that much sweeter.

Practice Makes Perfect

Golf is a great game, but it is a very selfish game. It lets you get out of it only as much as you put in, and to get the most out of it, you must put the time in practicing. Thinking about becoming a better player just won't get the job done.

But just like anything else, there are right ways and wrong ways to practice. You can spend hours beating range balls on the practice tee and all you'll have to show for it are blistered hands and swing flaws that are so deeply ingrained that it might well take brain surgery to get rid of them.

In this section I'd like to go over the best ways to practice, and also give you some suggestions to make practice not only more rewarding, but more enjoyable as well.

Pre-round Practice

I can't think of a single other sport that people try to play without warming up, and yet how often do you see people race to the first tee, pull out a driver and expect to play like the second coming of Bobby Jones? Plenty, I'd bet, and probably more often than you see people who take the time to properly prepare for a round.

Warming up before a round is important, if only because it can help prevent pulling muscles in your back, which comes under a lot of stress in the golf swing. But working your way through your bag before you play also gives you a chance to develop a good tempo, as well as finding the one or two swing keys that seem to work best for you that day. (See "My Swing Keys . . . and Yours," page 34.)

I always try to arrive at least forty-five minutes before my round. I don't want to get there too early because I'll wind up with time on my hands and my mind will start to wander away from the job at hand. You also want to guard against hitting too many practice balls. I've seen a lot of players go to town on the practice tee before their round, only to run out of gas by about the 15th hole.

The first thing I look for, after I've found a nice level area to practice from, is the direction of the wind. As much as possible, you want to practice into the wind because that will give you a truer reading of how your shots are flying. For example, let's say you get to the tee and the wind is quartering from the left to the right. If you just stand out there and stripe one beauty after another straight down the range, you may be in for a surprise when you get to the first hole and suddenly find that nice straight ball you were hitting on the tee was really a hook that the wind was holding up.

I like to start out with either my sand wedge or pitching wedge, hitting nice soft shots. I'm just trying to find a good tempo at this point, as well as develop a little feel.

Once I'm comfortable with these shots, I'll move through my set, skipping every other club until I get to the long irons and woods. I'll hit each club until I'm comfortable with it, and I'll always leave the club on a good shot. You don't want your last memory of a club to be a bad one when you need to hit it on the course. And just as on the course, you want to have a clear idea in mind for every shot.

Once I warm up, I'll try to hit a few different shots—high, low, fade and draw—just so I'm comfortable with the shots when I face them on the course. I'll also make a point of hitting several shots that are similar to the shots I'll face on the opening hole. It's a small thing, but it often gives you just the confidence you need to jump out to a fast start.

After I've worked my way through my clubs, I like to leave a few balls so I can "cool down" with some soft little wedge shots. It's one more way to make sure that you have all your ducks in a row when you start playing for real.

My final step before a round is to spend fifteen minutes or so on the practice green, hitting a few chips and pitches, and a lot of putts. I'm not worried as much about direction as I am about distance. I don't want to come out of the chute leaving myself a bunch of 3- and 4-footers to save par. You use up a lot of nerve early that way.

I want to stress, one more time, that the key to practicing before you play is getting yourself in the best physical and mental shape for your round. But there will be times when you get stuck in the office or one of the kids scrapes his knee at home, and you're going to come in sliding to the course without enough time to warm up correctly. When that's the case, here's my suggestion:

First, forget about hitting a bunch of clubs. Instead, hit several balls with a 5-iron, concentrating on finding a good tempo and at least one swing key that will help you stay in the game through the early holes, until you can play your way into shape. I like the 5-iron because it's what I call the "halfway club" in the set. It's halfway between the power clubs and the accuracy clubs, and you can hit every type of shot with it. In fact, I often suggest to people that they try playing a round with just a 5-iron, wedge and putter, since that will force them to invent all kinds of shots with the 5-iron they wouldn't ordinarily have to hit.

After you've hit as many balls as time allows, make a point of hitting at least a few putts and, hopefully, a couple chips. Not only will this give you a chance to develop some feel, but it will also help save some strokes on the early holes, when your game is bound to be rocky.

Finally, don't try to be a hero on the first hole. Forget the driver and maybe even the 3-wood. Just hit whatever you think you can get into play, even if that means hitting a 5-iron off the tee just to get a ball into play. Remember, you can always recover from a bogie, but starting out with a double, triple or worse can ruin your whole damn day.

Post-round Practice

The first thing to remember about practicing after a round is that you haven't got all day. You're bound to be physically tired and not all too sharp mentally. For that reason, I suggest you pick one problem area and try to figure out what's going wrong. It's also a good time to call in a professional, since the problem will be fresh in your mind, and easier for you and the pro to solve.

Once you've solved the problem, I suggest you call it a day. Experimenting when you're mentally and physically drained can only lead to disaster, which is why I think it's better to try to carve out some time just for practicing, both on and off the course.

And just a final reminder here: Don't forget to spend a few quiet minutes, before the end of the day, going over your round—charting where you wasted strokes, noting what swing thoughts worked best that day, and also making note of anything you noticed about the course that's worth remembering for future reference. The guys on tour have yardage books that they keep for each course, and they refer back to them year after year. Keeping such a book for your course would be a good idea.

Getting the Most from Practice

Like anything else, to get the most from practice you have to concentrate and have a plan of attack.

My first rule is that you must be very candid with yourself and identify both the strengths and weaknesses of your game. That's where charting your rounds can be so valuable. It's only human nature to want to practice what you can already do well, since it's a hell of a lot less work and a hell of a lot more fun. Sad to say, though, it doesn't do a lot to lower your handicap.

This is especially true if you're like most folks and spend strokes around the green the way a drunken sailor spends money in a liberty town. I know it's a lot more fun to stand out on the practice tee and rip drivers than it is to chip and pitch, or practice sand shots with the sand flying back in your face, but it all comes back to the question of how much you're willing to pay for success.

One solution might be to practice with a friend. Now I admit that most of your quality practice will come if you don't spend the time socializing, but I always enjoyed practicing with a friend—with a little something on the line, of course.

You can play closest to the hole with your chipping and pitching, or have a match around the putting clock for 25 cents a hole. Another good game is for each player to put three balls in a bunker and see how many strokes it takes to get all three balls up and down.

Another good game is a variation on the old schoolyard basketball game Horse, where players call the shot they plan to try. If the first player makes the basket, the other players have to make it as well, or they earn a letter. The first player to spell HORSE is out, and the last player wins.

In golf, you can go to the practice tee and call the shots you plan to hit to the different targets. Fade the first, draw the second and so on. To win, you not only have to hit the correct shot, but your ball must end up closest to the target. As I mentioned before, the best club for this game is a 5-iron, since you can hit the widest variety of shots with this club. Not only is this a good way to learn to hit a lot of shots, but it also teaches you to hit the shots under the pressure of competition.

On-course Practice

One of the best ways I know to practice is to forget the practice tee and green entirely and take your practice to the course. Very often in the summer it's possible to steal a little time early in the evening when the course isn't as crowded. This is the time you can really learn to play.

I suppose every kid who ever played this game has gone out and played three balls—one was his, the other two were those of two top players.

I must say, I was flattered when I heard that when he was a kid, Curtis Strange used to practice with three balls—Curtis against me and Ben Hogan. And when Tom Watson was in college at Stanford, he used to travel to Pebble Beach early in the morning and play two balls—him against Jack Nicklaus, coming down the final stretch in the U.S. Open. It's a little spooky when you realize that all that imagining came true back in 1982, when he beat Jack by making birdies on the last two holes to win the Open at Pebble Beach.

Here are three suggestions for games you can try when you're out on the course. And while they are really practice suggestions, you can also play them as a form of competition with a friend.

Go Way Back   Most of the time the vast majority of golfers never play from the back, or championship, tees. For one thing, they'd be out there all day, and for another, it just wouldn't be that much fun for them or their friends. Still, it's a good place to play an occasional practice round from if the course isn't crowded. By playing from the back tees, you wind up hitting a lot more fairway woods or long irons into the greens, both on approach shots and on par 3s. That's pretty good practice by itself, but since you'll wind up missing more greens, it's also a great way to improve your short game.

Play Your Worst Ball   There's a temptation when playing more than one ball to always play the best ball. What in the world does that do for you? I suggest you play two balls, always playing your next shot from where the worst ball lies. Not only will this improve your short game, but it will also help you develop the shots you need to scramble out of trouble, as well as teach you just how much you can realistically afford to gamble when in a jam.

Fade and Draw   This is really for the better players, since you need to be able to control the ball to make this pay off. The idea is to go out and fade one ball on each shot, while drawing the other. Not only will this improve your shotmaking skills, but it will also give you a real good idea of what type of shot you should be trying to hit under which circumstances.

Keeping Fit

As I've grown older, like most folks I've become more aware of how important exercise and nutrition really are. I've been blessed with pretty good health over the years, but I've also taken good care of myself, and there's no question that's a big reason I've been able to play as long and as well as I have. Early on, I saw a lot of talented players who were forced to leave the game, either because they got a bad break in the health department or because they ate and drank their way off the tour. I always felt bad for the guys in the first case and vowed to learn my lesson from the guys in the second.

As a kid I played so many sports, worked so hard around the farm, and did so much hunting and fishing, that I just naturally grew up to be pretty strong and supple. Of course, it didn't hurt that we Sneads came from pretty good breeding stock.

I'd like to clear up a misconception here and now. For years people have said that I'm double-jointed, which explained how I could pick a ball out of the cup without bending my knees or how until just recently I could kick the top of a doorway without my left foot leaving the ground.

In fact, at the 1979 PGA Championship I was heading toward the locker room when Gary Player saw me coming. He turned to a young pro and bet him that I could kick the top of the door. The kid's eyes lit up and he about had the money already spent before Gary even asked me to give it a try.

Well, I just stood there, gave it the old "one-two" and up my foot went just as easy as pie. Hell, if I had known there was money on the line, I would have tried to get a piece of it. I might have been able to get the ceiling. Come to think of it, I figure Gary still owes me a little something. After all, I did most of the work.

Anyway, the point of all this is that I'm not double-jointed, but I always have done a lot of stretching exercises to keep my muscles nice and oily. I suggest you do the same. In golf, you don't need hard muscles as much as you need supple strength.

Of course, you do need strong hands, especially when it comes to hitting short shots around the greens. I'll go on the record and say that the best shotmakers I've ever seen all had strong hands. In the old days, when pros apprenticed in shops, they developed that strength from playing, but also from working on clubs—rewhipping heads, wrapping grips and reshafting the old hickory clubs.

Today people don't get as much exercise as in the past, so I'd suggest doing anything you can to build up the strength in your hands, even if it means spending a few minutes each day squeezing tennis balls. I think it would be a good investment.

I'd also like to stress that walking is a great exercise for golf. As I said earlier, golf is a game that you play from the feet up, and if your legs are weak, they won't support your swing. I see middle-aged people, and even young folks, riding carts when they could be walking and I just shake my head. It's one of their few chances to get some exercise, and they spend it riding around, probably having a beer or two or three along the way. I don't call that golf. I call it cart-ball.

Now before anyone comes along and accuses me of being hypocritical, I'll admit that I ride nowadays, although J.C. is always after me to walk more. And I am trying because I do know that when my legs feel strong, I play better. But I'll just say that there's one hell of a lot of difference between a fellow riding at my age and someone half my age spending four or five hours bouncing around the countryside in a cart.

Eating and Drinking

I suppose you'd have had to be in a cave over the past few years to not know that science and medicine have come a long way in understanding what's good and bad for us. It used to be that when you said someone was a "meat and potatoes" guy it was a compliment. Now it seems that you're talking about a corpse in the making.

I don't pretend to be an expert on what food is or isn't good for you, but I know from experience that the right diet can improve your golf. Lord knows there are plenty of other books you can read that are about diets and whatnot.

I like a good piece of beef, but I tend to stick more to fish or chicken the night before a big round, because it's easier to digest.

Depending on what time you expect to play, you should plan your meals accordingly. If you have an early round, you should try to eat earlier in the evening so you'll be able to get a better night's sleep. I also think it's very important to avoid eating a big breakfast or lunch just before your round, since it tends to make you a little woozy or foggy.

During the round it's a good idea to drink plenty of water, especially it it's hot, since you need to guard against becoming dehydrated. Here's a warning: Drink a little bit of water on every tee if possible, rather than gulping down a lot of water every few holes. The idea is to replenish the water at the rate you're losing it.

It's also smart to carry snacks in your bag and eat them regularly throughout the round, rather than counting on a hot dog or some other snack at the turn. Crackers with peanut butter are good, and so are dried fruits or raisins. I avoid candy bars because the sugar makes my nerves twitchy.

Speaking of twitchy nerves brings me around to the three things that some people say will kill you, and I say will at least kill your chances for a decent score—tobacco, alcohol and caffeine.

I never really smoked, except for trying it as a kid. I didn't like the taste, and it made me so light-headed I thought I'd faint dead away on the spot. Even if I did smoke, I doubt I'd do it on the course, since it's one surefire way to tell if old man pressure is getting to you. It's a funny thing, but smokers tend to have a routine, and when they get tense, they really attack those cigarettes. People say they smoke to calm their nerves, but I doubt that's true. Either way, I'm not about to take it up and find out.

I was never much of a drinker, either. I might have an occasional beer or daiquiri, but never before a round or the night before. Alcohol gets to your system in a hurry and stays around for a long time before the effects truly wear off.

In all honesty, it's one of the things that always bothered me about pro-ams. I like to win, not just for the money involved, but for the sake of winning. Yet I'm out there playing my best, and there are guys who have been up partying all the night long, then stopping for a couple pops at the turn, who are supposed to be helping out the team. The truth is, I'd rather have a team of hackers who are sober and trying, than some low or middle handicappers out for a lark. I might not win with the hackers, but I damn sure know they were trying, and I've always been willing to help out guys who try. I've been known to lose my patience on occasion during a pro-am, but I don't think I ever got upset with a partner who was giving it his best shot.

What I've said about alcohol holds true to a lesser degree for caffeine, whether it's in coffee, tea or soft drinks. Caffeine has a different effect on everyone, but I know that it does give me just enough of the twitches that I'll avoid it if I can, especially the night before a match when I need a good night's sleep.

The Game Today

I think that golf is in better shape than at any time I can remember. More and more people are taking up the game. The pros are on television every weekend—the men's tour, the Senior Tour and the women's.

When you look at golfers compared with other athletes, there's no comparison. You never hear about golfers having drug problems or cheating or having run-ins with the law. That's the biggest reason so many companies like to get involved with golf. You can be sure it's not going to blow up in your face.

People say golfers are overpaid, but I don't agree. Compared with the other big sports like football, basketball and baseball, the top golfers don't begin to make what the top players in the other sports make. On top of that, there are no guaranteed contracts. If you don't play well on tour, you don't eat. It's that simple. And people don't

165

realize that golfers pay their own expenses, which run about $1,000 a week. If you miss the cut, your income for the week is a big fat zero.

I don't think that the best players today are any better than the best players in any other era. But I do know there is more depth on the tour now, and that will be even more true down the road. You see more and more of the better young athletes turning to golf, partially because the role models are so good compared to those of other sports.

So many good players are out there now that we need a second tour. The way the regular tour is structured now there's just not enough room for all the players. The new tour, which is being funded by Ben Hogan's golf company, will play smaller events in smaller cities. It will be a good place for the young guys to work on their games, for the guys who are struggling on the regular tour or some older guys who want to get ready to play the Senior Tour.

I think the big edge it will give us is that guys will learn to win. As the tour is set up now, it's hard for a young guy to get in contention, and you can't become a winner until you've been under the heat in the last round a few times. You have to learn to win out here, and the second tour will give the guys a chance to do just that.

I think that one reason foreign players like Seve, Greg Norman, Sandy Lyle, Bernhard Langer and Nick Faldo have done so well on our tour is that they got used to winning in Europe. Don't get me wrong, they're all wonderful players and would have done well here anyway, but they were comfortable with winning and had a lot of confidence when they arrived. That gave them a big edge.

I think another edge that the foreign players have is that they are a little hungrier than the Americans. It's almost as if they have a chip on their shoulders and want to prove how good they are. I wasn't very happy to see our boys lose the Ryder Cup, but I had to admire the spunk the Europeans showed. To be honest, I think they wanted to win a little bit more.

The foreign players are used to playing in tougher weather conditions and their courses aren't as well maintained. As a result, they get used to playing in adversity. When they arrive over here and see the perfectly maintained courses we have, they have a field day. I think that's one reason you see so many good young Americans struggle here, then play overseas for a while and come back as much better competitors. It toughens them.

But for all that, I think people who say that the foreign tours are as good as ours are nuts. I think the European tour is coming along, and the people over in Japan are crazy about the game, but our tour is still the best. If it wasn't, why would so many good foreign players be coming over here?

If there's one thing that could really hurt the growth of the game, it's the lack of courses. It used to be that cities and states would build courses, but now they're getting out of that, which is too bad. More and more courses are being plowed up and turned into shopping malls. My question is, where would you rather have your kids spend their time, on a course or wandering around a mall?

Of course, some of the new golf courses being built aren't any bargains either. Some of these so-called championship courses are a joke. They're just one long back-breaking hole after another, with mounds and railroad ties and all sorts of junk thrown all over the place. Compare that with a course like the Cascades, Pine Tree or Winged Foot and it will make you cry. By God, if I had to play a course like PGA West every day, I'd just up and quit this game altogether.

The problem is that everyone wants to outdo the fellow next door. Instead of building a subtle, shotmaker's course like Pinehurst #2 that you have to think your way around, all these architects are building courses that look like your worst nightmare come true. And what's worse, some of these courses are designed by good players, who ought to know better.

I do think that one change that would help would be rolling back the distance standard that the USGA applies to balls. The ball goes too far for the good players, and a lot of great courses have been made outdated. Merion is the best example. It's as good a course as you ever want to play, but now you can 1-iron it to death. Oakmont is another example. That course is a bear, but when the Open was played there in 1983, Seve Ballesteros practically left his driver in the bag. That's not right. One of the beauties of golf is seeing how players from one generation to the next compare when they play the same courses. We're losing that today.

For all the changes, golf is still the best sport of them all. You compete with yourself, the course and the other players. You meet nice folks and you can play all your life. And you never stop learning.

I've had a great run. I've been treated well. I've taken a lot from the game and I like to think I've given back a fair amount, too.

People ask if I'd trade it all in for another go-around. I don't know. I wouldn't change my swing and I'm pretty damn proud of my record. If I could go at it with the knowledge I have now, maybe I'd be tempted.

Of course, if I was sure I'd make just a few more putts. . . .

Index